EVERYTHING
I KNOW ABOUT
BUSINESS
I LEARNED FROM
THE GODFATHER

EVERYTHING
I KNOW ABOUT
BUSINESS
I LEARNED FROM
THE GODFATHER

ROBERT GORE

Dedication

To Enzo the baker, the only true hero in The Godfather

Preface

Writing about *The Godfather*'s business lessons is not an endorsement of horses' heads in beds, garroting, cold-blooded murders of business rivals, bribery, extortion, or any other Mafia criminality, any more than writing about the US government is an endorsement of theft via taxation, regulatory extortion, crony socialism, regime changes, senseless and endless wars, intelligence agency skullduggery, Orwellian surveillance, bureaucratic rot, and nonstop lies. Discuss the former and you're a Mafia apologist. Embrace the latter and you're a paid up member of one of the two major political parties. It's all part of the same hypocrisy.

The Godfather, novel and movies, is about a *business*, the Corleone Mafia "family." It offers lessons about business not found in business school texts or the rest of the vast and often useless literature devoted to the subject

The Godfather is not an accurate representation of the Mafia. Real life mafiosi do not have the majesty of Don Vito Corleone, nor the operatic pathos of his youngest son's arc in life. According to a *Life* magazine fifty-year retrospective on the book and movies, Mario Puzo had no experience with the Mafia and got most of his material from library research.

It's quite true that a movie like *Goodfellas* far better captures the unappealing reality of the Mafia. It's also quite true that no Mafia book or movie has come close to capturing the popular imagination like *The Godfather*.

Lines have become instantly recognized expressions in the common vernacular. Scenes—the wedding, Jack Woltz's bedroom, Luca Brasi's garroting, Clemenza telling Lampone to take the cannoli, the causeway massacre, the baptism, the contentious meeting between Michael and Senator Geary, Michael's kiss of death for Fredo, Hyman Roth gunned down at the airport—have become iconic imprints on the collective consciousness. Every Mafia book, movie, and TV series owes an often acknowledged debt to *The Godfather*. It dwarfs its successors and imitators. There will be no glossy fifty-year retrospectives for *Goodfellas*.

Complaints about inauthenticity are like complaints that *Hamlet* is inaccurate history: true, but irrelevant. Both are transcendent works of art, for which reality is a platform, to be used and embellished for the sake of their authors' stories and truths. That both endure suggests that those stories and truths have struck deep, responsive chords within the human psyche.

My sources for this book were the novel, *The Godfather Part One*, *Part Two* and *Part Three* movies, and the *Life* retrospective. I've read the book maybe ten times and seen the *Parts One* and *Two* around fifteen times apiece. Obviously they struck chords in my psyche. I didn't like *Part Three* as well and mention it infrequently.

I've said very little about myself or my book in this preface. I'm hoping you're not expecting much. The reasons for both will become clear when you read Chapter Five. By the end of the book, you may have picked up a thing or two about business, life, and why *The Godfather* resonates so deeply.

One final note: this book can be enjoyably and profitably read by those who have never read *The Godfather* or seen the movies, and especially by those who don't like standard business books.

Acknowledgments

I am grateful to my wife, Roberta, who has always supported my writing, and my son, Austin, who has watched *The Godfather* movies with me many times and has contributed valuable insights.

I am grateful to Holly Ollivander, who had the idea for this book and encouraged me to write it, edited it, designed the cover, and helped with other design elements.

I am also grateful to Mario Puzo, G. P. Putnam's Sons Publishing, Francis Ford Coppola, Albert S. Ruddy, Paramount Pictures, Alfran Productions, The Coppola Company, American Zoetrope and Zoetrope Studios, Marlon Brando, Al Pacino, Robert Duvall, James Caan, Diane Keaton, Richard S. Castellano, Abe Vigoda, Talia Shire, Gianni Russo, John Cazale, Robert De Niro, Lee Strasberg, Nino Rota and the rest of the cast and production teams that made *The Godfather* novel and films enduring classics.

A Note on Terminology

The following Italian terms are used throughout this book (spellings are taken from *The Godfather*):

Consigliori: The counselor and right-hand man to the Don, who is the head of the family.

Caporegime: Often shortened to *capo;* a ranking member of a Mafia family who has "made his bones," heads a "crew" of soldiers, and has major status and influence within the family.

Omerta: The Sicilian code of silence.

Pezzonovantis: Big shots, the people who run things, the powers that be.

The following shorthand is used to denote the novel and the movies:

The Godfather: *The Godfather* novel, by Mario Puzo, G. P. Putnam's Sons, 1969.

Part One: the movie *The Godfather, Part One*, Paramount Pictures and Alfran Productions, 1972.

Part Two: the movie *The Godfather, Part Two*, Paramount Pictures, The Coppola Company, and American Zoetrope, 1974.

Part Three: the movie *The Godfather, Part Three,* Paramount Pictures and Zoetrope Studios, 1990.

If I can prevent one person from attending business school, my work here is done.

Chapter 1

It's Business, Not Personal

The light flashed on the phone board. It was an internal line. I picked it up.

"Bob, can you meet me in the conference room?" It was Andrew, my boss.

"Sure, I'll be there in a minute."

I was about to be fired.

In 1990, Andrew's father, Don, hired me to run the fixed income department of a Southern California securities firm, a private partnership. I became one of the firm's youngest partners and eventually a member of the executive committee. Don and I had been close friends. He died in 2004 and Andrew took over as the managing partner. We weren't close, but we had a cordial working relationship.

For twenty-two years I ran the fixed income department and traded municipal bonds, almost always profitably. In 2005, I saw the housing meltdown coming. We sold my family's home in early 2006, close to the top of the market. I wanted to place a big bet on deteriorating credit quality and a financial crisis. Not on the scale of the heroes of *The Big Short*, but the same general idea. Andrew gave me permission.

In 2007 I set up an offshoot to the fixed income department, a proprietary trading desk that would speculate not just in bonds, but futures, commodities, currencies, and swaps. I was particularly interested in credit default swaps, esoteric financial instruments that were essentially bets on the credit quality of a corporation or government.

I hired an experienced credit default swaps trader and another trader. Like a big hedge fund, we set up a prime brokerage account with one of the Wall Street firms. I quit trading municipal bonds to oversee the operation.

It worked. In 2008, a year in which virtually every bank and Wall Street firm lost money and many of them either went out of business or would have except for government bailouts, our little proprietary trading desk made a bundle on the financial meltdown. Much of the profits came from owning credit default swaps—bearish credit-quality bets—on those banks and Wall Street firms.

Unfortunately, we left a lot of money on the table. When Lehman Brothers failed we feared our Wall Street prime broker would be next. I couldn't risk it going bankrupt, taking our money with it. We closed out our trades and pulled our funds just as those trades were skyrocketing in value, driven by financial crisis panic. Not that we didn't make a nice piece of change, but our prime broker got bailed out and we would have made a lot more if we hadn't sold our positions.

We also made a nice piece of change in municipal bonds. My hand-picked replacement as the head municipal bond trader quit in October and I went back to trading municipal bonds, just in time for a spectacular and rewarding rally.

At the annual partners' meeting early the next year, I bragged that the firm had made more money than the major Wall Street firms combined, because they had all reported huge losses. I was warmly applauded.

Ah, hubris. Your worst trades often follow your best ones. In retrospect, I should have announced at the partners' meeting that I was quitting, but what trader, or gambler of any stripe, goes out on top?

Around that time the stock market hit its low. Our proprietary trading desk stayed bearish and started taking substantial losses. Municipal bond trading was still profitable, but I let the losses in proprietary trading go on for too long. Like a desperate gambler who thinks he's going to get his losses back, I didn't stop my traders who were losing money, hoping their luck would change. It didn't. After almost two years I finally fired them.

In 2011, I hired a trader of esoteric mortgage derivatives. My first mistake was not understanding what he was trading. My second mistake was ignoring my own gut instincts, which said he was too nice a guy to be a trader. As a rule, good traders are contrarians who despise the crowd, not nice guys. The trader booked a profit for 2011, but his portfolio valuations were based on estimates from the street that weren't "real" bids that would be good for a trade. There was no public market for what he was trading.

Early in 2012, his market headed south and he started taking losses. Not understanding what he was trading or how the instruments were valued, I had to take his word for valuations, which he got from other traders of the same securities. By summer, I knew we were in trouble. During a vacation, I decided I had to take the bull by the horns. When I got back to work, I told the trader to give me an estimate of the total loss if we sold all his positions.

It was a big number, which I reported to Andrew. He was dismayed and told me to close out the positions. We did so, and the total loss came in over twice what the trader had estimated. When I saw it, I knew the trader and I were through.

A few days later, I went to the conference room for my meeting with Andrew. It wasn't going to be pleasant. We made some nervous small talk.

"Bob," he said, coming to the preordained point, "I have to ask you for your resignation."

When you get high enough in business, they don't fire you, they ask for your resignation. Nobody is fooled, but "he resigned" sounds better than "he was fired." There are legal differences between the two. I was eligible for a severance payment, which I wouldn't have been if I was officially "fired," but in my mind I was fired.

"You can have my resignation, but did you talk to people in the firm about this?" I thought I had support within the firm. Through the years I had made a lot of people, especially the partners, significant money. "Maybe think about it over the weekend."

It was late Friday afternoon. I'll bet 90 percent of firings happen on late Friday afternoons. Managers stall on firings because they're unpleasant, but they don't like them hanging over their weekends. Despite my suggestion, I knew that having mustered the gumption to fire me, Andrew wasn't going to change his mind.

"Could you stay on for the next six weeks?" he asked. "Do whatever it takes to get things squared away in your operation?"

"Sure."

This was completely contrary to usual Wall Street practice. They fire you and they want you out the door—immediately. I think I smiled. Here was a guy I had cost a lot of money asking me to stay on and put things right. And here was the guy who had just been fired agreeing to do so. In *The Godfather's* memorable phrase, it was business, not personal.

Since man first evolved, or was created or intelligently designed, he's formed groups. Not just because he's a social animal, but because it furthers a common interest in survival. Have you ever tried to kill a woolly mammoth by yourself? It wouldn't be easy, even with firearms, and it was even harder for cavemen with spears and clubs. So they banded together, and if their luck was running right, they got the mammoth. If not, the mammoth got them.

Nothing is more important to a man than what he must do to survive. Nowadays it's fashionable for men to say that nothing is more important to them than their families, but if a man can't survive he certainly can't support a family. For centuries supporting and protecting his family has been the essential test of manhood, a duty approached with the utmost seriousness. Now we see plenty of men who don't work or support their family. An unanswered question, because asking it upsets the proper-think *pezzonovantis* (big shots): what does it do to men who rely on someone else for their own and their family's support?

Men turn to groups and the advantages they offer for collective survival. Every group has rules and a hierarchy, a structure to run things. For the group to survive and flourish, its rules must align with the purposes of the group and the challenges it faces. Those running the group must enforce them. Violating the rules is one thing and must be punished, but there are some violations that amount to a betrayal of the group or its core tenets and beliefs, posing a threat to its members and perhaps its very existence.

Nobody is 100 percent right on markets. Every trader and trading unit occasionally loses money. Any firm that wants to stay in business can't permit traders to decide how much money they'll be allowed to lose. Any trader who has made a lot of money can lose just as much or more, and there's always a loss so large it will get the trader fired. It's an occupational hazard, but losses are business, not personal.

A trader under my authority had lost a lot of money, enough to hit Andrew's pain point. I had screwed up, not understanding what that trader was trading, not having any independent way to value his positions. However, I hadn't betrayed Andrew or the company. I had been the one who forced the issue, insisting on an estimate of the trader's losses and reporting them to Andrew. In all the years I had worked there, I had never "desk-drawered," or hidden, positions or losses. I had been straight up with Don and then Andrew, and with the firm's other partners.

My transgressions were business mistakes, but I had always acted honorably. Andrew recognized that, or he wouldn't have asked me to stay on. I wanted to make amends or I wouldn't have agreed. I wasn't going to act like some jilted lover and storm out of the conference room. It was business, not personal.

"Leave the gun. Take the cannoli."

—*Part One*

It could have been worse. I could have been Paulie Gatto.

Betrayal is always personal. Corleone justice was severe, but the rules were clear. Three bullets in the back of the head may seem harshly unfair to those who know little of the world or its history. Betrayal of the group or its leaders often exacts the supreme penalty. Religions have executed those who renounced the faith. Armies put spies and deserters before firing squads.

Betrayal can be a matter of life or death. Gatto's almost cost the Godfather his life and the Corleone family its very existence. He plunged the five New York families into a bloody and disastrous war from which the Corleones emerged victorious only after Sonny was murdered, and Michael killed Sollozzo and the police captain, endured exile to Sicilily, and watched his wife get blown up.

Sonny wasn't a good don, but his justice for Gatto was textbook correct. The execution was swift, sure, and public.

> *But it had to be public so that embryo traitors would be frightened and the enemy warned that the Corleone Family had by no means gone stupid or soft. Sollozzo would be made wary by this quick discovery of his spy. The Corleone Family would win back some of its prestige. It had been made to look foolish by the shooting of the old man.*

> *—The Godfather*

Sonny offers a lesson to those who must fire people. One of my biggest failures as a manager was that I took too long to do it. Managers tend to have an inflated opinion of their ability to turn poor performers into competent ones. I know I did. It's pure ego. My failing was endemic to the firm. People repeatedly got away with things that should have gotten them canned. Bad as my record was, I had fired more people than anyone else in the firm.

When people aren't making the grade, the chances of turning those situations around are slim. Get rid of them, sooner rather than later. If their behavior has been dishonorable, take it personally. Maybe don't shoot them three times in the back of the head, but fire immediately, file criminal charges if warranted, and make sure everyone within the company knows that punishment was swift, sure, and appropriate.

Within a year after I left the firm, it was sold at a distress price to another company after sustaining substantial losses. That's what happens when you don't get rid of your losers.

Chapter 2

Respect

Respect is the lifeblood of any organization. People inside and outside the organization have to respect its purposes, leadership, and way it conducts itself. Drain that lifeblood and the organization dies.

"Godfather" and "Don Corleone" were titles of respect for a man even his enemies respected. Part of that was based on fear, but it didn't stem solely from the Don's ruthlessness and propensity for violence. Sonny was more ruthless and violent, but less respected. The Godfather took respect for himself and his family as his due, but unlike Sonny he had the qualities of personality and character that commanded it. Much of *The Godfather* is the family's effort to regain lost respect, for which Sonny was primarily responsible.

Americans have always loved the classic rags-to-riches American success story, especially that of an off-the-boat immigrant. The self-made man is our heroic archetype. Nine-years-old, both parents murdered by a

Sicilian don, Vito Corleone arrives steerage-class at Ellis Island, the Statue of Liberty in the background. He and his fellow immigrants gaze with wonder and hope at this symbol of their new country.

Part Two and the novel trace Vito's self-made evolution from grocery store delivery boy to proprietor of Genco Pura Olive Oil company and head of the most powerful Mafia family in New York. Amazingly, he achieves all this without an MBA—indeed with no formal education of any kind! (If you look up the histories of America's financial and industrial titans, you'll find that many of them didn't have much in the way of formal education.)

If that were all there was to the Godfather, his story would only rate a feature in organized crime's equivalent of *Forbes.* What lifts him above the run-of-the-mill success story is his dispensation of justice. The first character we meet is Amerigo Bonasera, whose belief in America has been shattered and who has come to the Godfather to plead for the justice and vengeance denied him by the judicial system.

In virtually every religion, a vital function of the god or gods is to dispense justice. Unlike the gods, the Godfather never disappoints.

And then, no matter how poor or powerless the supplicant, Don Corleone would take that man's troubles to his heart. And he would let nothing stand in the way to a solution of that man's woe.

—The Godfather

A longing for justice is hard-wired into humanity's DNA. Is there anyone who doesn't find the brutal "justice" administered by Corleone strong-arms to the two punks who terrorized Bonasera's daughter immensely satisfying?

Cluck all you want about extra-judicial recourse and violence, but the money and political influence that kept such scum out of prison were also extra-judicial. Did they deserve their freedom or to be left as bloody pulps on a New York sidewalk? That most people choose the latter helps explain *The Godfather's* enduring appeal. Who hasn't felt the frustration and rage of injustice inflicted by unaccountable and invulnerable power and longed for Godfather-style retribution?

The Corleone family was built on the Don's business and organizational skills, negotiating acumen, vision, ingenuity, guts, ruthlessness, terror, and political power. Within the family, respect and loyalty were owed not just to his formidable personage, but to all of one's superiors and peers, the family's rules, and Mafia traditions—notably *omerta*, the code of silence. The penalties for disrespect were harsh, up to and including execution.

Don Corleone knew that respect and loyalty had to run both ways. He treated top hit man Luca Brasi with "regal respect." Family members serving prison time received a living allowance if they kept their mouths shut. When they were released, there was a homecoming party, a personal welcome and thanks from an important family figure—maybe even the Don—and money for a vacation before they started back to work.

Loyalty was stringently enforced but faithfully rewarded.

Early in *Part One*, the Don, Sonny, and *Consigliori* Tom Hagen discuss an upcoming meeting with Virgil Sollozzo and his proposition for the family to enter the drug trade. Sonny and Hagen give their opinions, which they know are contrary to the Don's predisposition, and he listens respectfully.

Towards the end of *Part One*, *Caporegimes* Clemenza and Tessio voice their displeasure at the strategy being pursued by the semiretired Don and Michael. Clemenza even asks to form his own family. The Godfather refuses, but neither *caporegime* is upbraided for speaking his piece. The Don was an absolute ruler but not an insecure one. He listened to other points of view and tolerated dissent from those he trusted and respected.

Of course, once decisions were made everyone was expected to close ranks.

> *"Santino, come here! What's a matter with you? I think your brain is going soft from all that comedy you're playing with that young girl. Never tell anybody outside the family what you're thinking again!"*

—*Part One*

Sonny's failure to close ranks would cost the family dearly.

Modern CEOs praise their employees' loyalty and brag about consulting with them, announce to the board of directors and shareholders that they're cutting jobs, then bemoan the pervasive lack of respect for executives and profess not to be able to understand its source.

Jack Woltz, the studio owner who woke up with a horse's head in his bed, said a man in his position could not "afford to be made to look ridiculous." He was right. For an organization to be respected, its leader must convey an essential dignity, a word that's gone out of style.

You can count on one hand the number of jokes in *The Godfather* and the movies. The Mafia is a serious business. Anyone approaching it or its members flippantly would be demonstrating disrespect, and would in turn be disrespected and ostracized, or worse. Don Corleone tells Virgil Sollozzo he's agreed to see him because he heard that Sollozzo was "a serious man, to be treated with respect." Seriousness of purpose and respect are inseparable.

The biggest off-balance sheet asset of any business is its reputation, which starts at the top and flows downward. I go to business conferences and hear executive presentations about how committed companies are to "sustainability," "saving our planet," "our children," "stakeholders," "good corporate citizenship," "diversity," and so on, a laundry list of words and phrases approved by the proper-think *pezzonovantis*. Profits are seldom mentioned.

The PR and genuflecting before current political totems are easy substitutes for the very hard work of acting honorably and maintaining a reputation for competence, integrity and fair dealing, acknowledging and correcting mistakes, and selling services and products that provide honest value at a profit to the company.

Whatever goodwill that accrues from the PR and genuflecting is vanquished in an instant when a business and its leaders are discovered to have acted dishonorably. The proper-think *pezzonovantis* don't believe it, but most people aren't stupid, they see through pretense. The wages of hypocrisy are contempt. Hypocrisy is rampant in American business, and so too is contempt for it. Once lost, no amount of PR can restore respect.

Before I entered the private partnership, I worked at the Los Angeles office of a Wall Street firm. I was consistently appalled by the shenanigans I witnessed there. It was one of the reasons I eventually left, even though the private partnership was smaller, less prestigious, and initially less remunerative.

The people running corporations are shielded by corporations' legal "personhood," which means that when corporations commit crimes or regulatory infractions, the corporation and not the individuals responsible are charged, prosecuted, and punished—usually payment of a fine. Corporate limited liability laws also mean that the shareholder-owners' assets are protected—their liability is limited to the amount they have invested in the corporation.

In a private partnership, the partners' money and reputations are on the line *and* all of the partners' assets outside the partnership are at risk. Do something bad and an aggrieved party can come after your house. You can be tossed in jail. It produces an entirely different ethic. Not surprisingly, almost all the old line Wall Street partnerships converted to corporations. My firm was a holdout.

Partnerships are more cautious, more disposed to compromise and settle with aggrieved parties and, I would argue, more ethical than corporations. Our private partnership was known as squeaky clean, a reputation we maintained all the years I worked there. I'm proud of whatever part I played in that.

It's not just business that's held in contempt. You'd be hard-pressed to name an institution in American life that isn't, or to argue that they don't deserve it.

The government extracted over $3 trillion from taxpayers in 2018 but still managed to run a deficit close to $1 trillion. It's over $22 trillion in the hole. If it had to account for its pension and medical liabilities in the way it requires for private businesses, its liabilities would be five to ten times that number, depending on who's doing the estimating. It's bankrupt, and only the central bank conjuring unlimited credit to buy its debt keeps the charade going.

The same people who have turned the government into a fiscal derelict think they ought to run the rest of the world, too. Only in the public sector: if at first you don't succeed, go on to a bigger job. Around $1 trillion a year is spent on the military and intelligence services that haven't won a war since World War II, but have spawned chaos, carnage, and hatred towards the US across the globe.

The rest of the world is finally getting the message: the US is a paper tiger. Every day brings a new challenge to the crumbling empire and its regime. At home, all we have from our wars are legions of physically and psychologically broken veterans, tombstones and monuments for the dead, and a huge, unpaid bill.

Ringo Starr said, "Everything government touches turns to crap." The government now touches everything, even kids' lemonade stands, and you can't help but step in the crap. It's squeezing the life out of the country. Hard to believe, but many people want it to touch still more, to tighten its chokehold.

The latest fiasco is Obamacare, which may single-handedly reverse the long-running trend of rising life expectancy in this country. I won't catalogue its many shortcomings and woes; I'll only recount my own experience with it.

After I became self-employed in 2012, my family's medical insurance was under $500 a month. For a 2018 policy that wasn't as good as my 2012 policy, I would have had to pay over $1600 a month. The deductible was $12,000—more than twice what it was in 2012. I would be out over $30,000 before the insurance company paid for anything but my family's check-ups and prescriptions. Here's more salt in the wound: the money I spent would have indirectly subsidized other people's insurance and medical care.

I didn't buy insurance in either 2018 or 2019. Expensive as things are, thirty grand would pay for a gall bladder and a hernia operation—should such medical misfortunes befall my family—with some left over. For costlier maladies I just have to risk it. Cancer would wipe us out. I have many strongly held emotions about Obamacare and the politicians who foisted it on us. None of those emotions remotely resembles respect. I am happy, however, that I'm not subsidizing anyone else's medical care, especially the freeloading scum who say it's my duty to pay for that or any other socialist "entitlement."

The government has turned us into a nation of those who make the money and those who take it from them, with government being the biggest taker. The Washington area is the wealthiest in the country, a vipers' nest of politicians, bureaucrats, contractors, corporations, lawyers, lobbyists, and other criminals contesting for their unfair share of the $4 plus trillion the government now spends every year.

Donald Trump's real running mate in 2016 was Contempt, the contempt millions of Americans have for the government and what it does. Like or hate Trump, it's clear that such contempt isn't going away and will undoubtedly intensify. Future candidates will either capitalize on it, as Trump has, or be buried by it.

Don Corleone believed he ran his world much better than the *pezzonovantis* ran the outside world. He wasn't wrong, and that was back in the 1940s, when the government was smaller, less intrusive, and could do something right, like win a war.

Thomas Jefferson thought the press should and would be a thorn in the government's side. That's not how things have worked out. Aside from Internet rebels, the media is the fourth branch of government. It reliably spouts the government's line and its leading figures shamelessly suck up to the politicians The government's long slide in public trust and esteem has been matched by the media's and for many of the same reasons.

As with the media, Hollywood, sports, and academia have become bastions of proper-think and proper-speak, given over to indoctrination and reform of the reactionary and benighted. Once upon a time, celebrities and professors were almost universally admired. Now a good many of them are best-case ignored, worst-case despised by those of us who don't play at games or do make-believe for a living.

With incomes and sinecures far surpassing what they could earn in honest work, clueless celebrities and academics drip condescension as they lecture the masses on our myriad faults. In the throes of delusional righteousness, they proclaim their devotion to the less fortunate and *demand* the adoption of their schemes to save our "imperiled" planet, all of which involve ever-expanding and invasive government.

Lest you think you'll find some solace from all this in organized religion, that churches are worthy of respect, think again. The Catholic church is and will be undone for many decades by the pedophilia it condoned. It doesn't help its cause that the Pope spouts more proper-speak than Scripture. There he's joined by many on the Protestant side of the Reformation split. For much of organized Christianity, salvation supposedly depends on political choices.

I recently attended a "Celebration of a Life," what used to be called a funeral or memorial service, at a "progressive" Protestant church. The woman who died was a close friend of my mother. She was in her mid-eighties, but sharp as a tack and in full control of her faculties until she fell down a flight of stairs. The accident greatly impaired her cognitive and intellectual capacities and several months afterward she died. Had it not happened, she might have gone on living a full life for many more years.

You would have thought the service was a wedding, everyone was so damn happy. My mom was devastated by her friend's death, but she and the woman's maid shed the only tears I saw in that church. A woman sitting next to my mom, a long-time friend of both my mom and the dead woman, insisted that I take a picture of her and my mom. She instantly summoned an impressive smile. After I took the picture and showed it to her, she was upset with mom for her tears and for looking sad!

I don't usually cry on such occasions, but I felt the woman's memory deserved a show of somber respect. Has paying such respect gone completely out of style? The service was as genuine and meaningful as a happy-face emoticon. The woman leading the service was a proper-speak robot, a walking, talking opioid. She assured us that it was "okay" to feel sad about the death. I'm sure that was a comfort to my mom. Everything was positive, uplifting, upbeat, and life affirming, any grief or mourning a passing affectation only.

Even if one believes in an afterlife, departing this one should elicit sorrow and fond remembrance. A friend to whom I wrote about the service wrote back.

...the shortest and most concise verse in The Gospels is, Jesus wept, *which he did, and heartily, upon encountering his dead kinsman Lazarus. Even though he had the power to raise him from the dead* he still took the time to grieve.

You may ask: if respect is the lifeblood of an institution, and if all of our institutions command contempt rather than respect, does that mean they will all eventually die? You've answered your own question.

Even the dead and their memories are no longer respected. Unlike most of what is no longer respected, the dead deserve better.

Chapter 3

"You Can Act Like A Man!"

The most difficult respect is self-respect. If you don't respect yourself, you won't respect anyone or anything else, and no one will respect you.

Thousands of articles, books and videos purport to show people how they can respect themselves. Such works wouldn't find the audience they do if people didn't see significant shortcomings in the way they think, feel, behave, or interact with other people. The feel-better-about-yourself corpus addresses a fundamental and pervasive lack of self-respect. Unfortunately for those so beset, the remedy is rarely found in such works. Nevertheless, many of the chronically insecure acquire libraries of them, bouncing from one can't miss formula to another.

The Godfather ties self-respect inextricably to a self-control that would gladden the heart of an old-fashioned Puritan. Modern culture screams: indulge, indulge, indulge. *The Godfather* screams: repress, repress, repress.

Repression is now considered a psychological malady. By today's standards, Don Vito (played by John Belushi) required the psychiatric group therapy he received in the famous *Saturday Night Live* sketch. He's a study in repression and so is Michael.

It's a testament to their skills as actors that Marlon Brando and Al Pacino made their faces such impassive masks that the smallest twitch or movement sufficed to convey an emotion or thought. Slightly raised eyebrows signal Vito's nonchalance upon learning the grisly fates of Khartoum and Jack Woltz. It's another man's minor incident at the office.

Michael's cold stare and quiet forcefulness are more intimidating than an offended Sicilian father who—flanked by his sons—is determined to defend the honor of daughter Apollonia. Gathering his rifle and about to flee, bodyguard Fabrizzio, on an order from Michael, reverses course and summons the father. Michael stays in his chair, as relaxed and dangerous as a rattlesnake sunning itself on a warm rock.

Self-control was at the core of the two Dons' strength and force of personality. Control of self is required for control or power over others. It's necessary to command respect, and it's necessary to surmount the challenges and fulfill the responsibilities that come with being the head of a Mafia family.

If Michael had stumbled drunk into his and Kay's bedroom, would he have had the presence of mind to look out the bedroom window, duck for cover, and shield Kay from the killers who opened fire from outside? Old as Don Corleone was, as soon as he saw the gunmen sent to kill him he ran towards his car.

Although he was badly wounded, that response saved his life. Every day a don gambles with his life. Playing the percentages and split-second responses demand sobriety and ever-alert focus.

Most leaders don't have to worry about being killed. However, business executives are under constant pressure to think, plan, implement, react quickly and appropriately to unexpected contingencies, and improvise. They must obtain the respect of those they lead, respect which can be destroyed in an instant by their own words and actions. There is more margin for error than that enjoyed by Corleone father and son, but not much. A mistake may not cost them their lives, but it can cost them their job or their company.

It's not playing the percentages for people in such positions to diminish their capacities in any way; the stakes are too high. The Corleone dons are models of sobriety and rectitude. (Talk about a word that's out of fashion!) They have the occasional glass of wine, an integral part of Italian culture. Other than that, they drink infrequently. Vito smokes a cigar now and then. He's "notoriously straitlaced" in matters of sex. Neither he nor Michael cheat on their wives.

Hagen said quietly, "I didn't tell Mama anything. I was about to come up and wake you and tell you the news myself. In another moment I would have come to waken you."

Don Corleone said impassively, "But you needed a drink first."

"Yes," Hagen said.

"You've had your drink," the Don said. "You can tell me now." There was the faintest hint of reproach for Hagen's weakness.

—*The Godfather*

In matters of personal comportment, *Consigliori* Tom Hagen is on the same straight and narrow as Vito and Michael Corleone, but *any* weakness must be guarded against, even the weakness that requires a drink before Don Vito is told his oldest son is dead.

Avoiding vices and illicit sexual liaisons didn't just demonstrate the Dons' strength and preserve their energy and focus. The rules of their world were far more stringent, and the penalties for violations far more severe, than those of the wider world around them Dissipation drains and eventually destroys integrity, character, and judgment. Veracity and trustworthiness are the first casualties of dissolution, as countless relatives and friends of alcoholics, addicts, and philanderers can attest. A don who makes promises he doesn't keep, refuses to stand by his commitments, and lies to those upon whom he must rely is not long for this world.

In *Part Two*, young Vito tells Clemenza and Tessio that he never lies to his friends. This implies that it's acceptable to lie to one's enemies, in the same way warring countries peddle disinformation and fake intelligence to their enemies. Of course, should enemies prevail in either instance, the liar will face execution.

Although he becomes known as a man of his word, Vito demonstrates a lawyerly skill in shading the truth,

25

even to his friends. In *Part Two*, Clemenza asks him if he looked in a bag of guns that Clemenza gave him. Vito did, but instead of admitting to it, responds, "I'm not interested in things that don't concern me." Not technically a lie, since a bag of perhaps illicit guns in his possession is undoubtedly a matter of concern, but definitely not the whole truth. Clemenza doesn't quite know what to make of that answer, but doesn't press the issue.

The Godfather's pledge in *Part One*, that "by the souls of my grandchildren" (the souls of his children may have already been pledged) he will not break the peace arranged among the nation's dons is at best a half-truth. Perhaps he doesn't, technically, but Michael does, and father helps son plan the bloodbath. They would argue that the misleading pledge falls within the lying-to-the-enemy exception.

A world in which "likes" and not respect are the coin of the realm would be completely alien to *Godfather* soldiers and capos. That anyone would attach any significance to strangers' or even friends' "likes" on a social media platform would strike them as a mentally unbalanced display of immaturity and insecurity. Self-respecting Mafiosi couldn't afford to look immature or insecure, they had to be their own men. It's inconceivable that Vito or Michael would care whether anyone liked them, irrelevant foolishness. They were to be respected, not liked.

Vito, Michael, and Tom Hagen are paragons of self-control and self-respect, and they live long and prosper. The flip side of this morality tale: those unable to overcome their self-destructive predilections come to bad ends.

In *Part One,* we meet Fredo Corleone at his sister's wedding. He's drunk. Introduced to Michael and Kay, he radiates the kind of supplicating affection that gets dogs scratched behind the ears.

Later, after a nervous breakdown from seeing his father shot, Fredo, or Freddie, is sent to Las Vegas—Sin City—where, by his father's lights, he sins.

Freddie had proved to be nothing more than an innkeeper and ladies' man, the idiom for ladies' man untranslatable but connoting a greedy infant always at its mother's nipple—in short, unmanly.

—The Godfather

Fredo becomes a "lackey" of both women and hot-headed gangster Moe Greene. Taking two women to bed at the same time is "degeneracy." Allowing Moe Greene to slap him around in public is far worse—a disrespectful insult to Fredo and the entire Corleone family. Fredo compounds his woes by cravenly sticking up for Greene, which elicits a severe rebuke and warning from Don-in-waiting Michael.

"Fredo, you're my older brother and I love you, but don't ever take sides with anyone against the family again. Ever."

—Part One

In *Part Two*, Fredo disregards the warning and completes the arc begun in *Part One*. He betrays Michael and the family, and although "he's weak and he's stupid" (Michael's words), and "helpless" (Connie's word), Michael has him murdered. The wages of degeneracy and cowardice are fratricide.

Way back when, the more astute woolly mammoth hunters noticed that the mammoths were unconcerned with their feelings. Angry, frustrated, or despondent as they might get, the mammoths didn't care. In fact, most of their emotions—other than the thrill of the hunt—were a hindrance and made their job harder to do. Generalizing, reality didn't care about their emotions, only about how well the tribesmen grasped and used it to improve their situation.

Emotional repression was not just something men did because of bad parenting or because all the other men were doing it. They did it because reality demanded it. Thousands of generations later, reality still demands that those engaged in designing microchips, finding a cure for cancer, or any of the other endeavors that spell human progress put their emotions aside and fully engage their rationality and logic. Displays of emotion meet with reality's disdain.

When I was trading, I trained myself to maintain a poker face and flatten my emotional graph as much as I could. I did the same in basketball games after work. No bragging about the wins, no bemoaning the losses, they were yesterday's trade, or game—water under the bridge—and you had to focus on the next one, not the last one. Trading and basketball are competitive and you do what you can to gain an edge, including hiding your emotions.

It's a discipline no one completely masters, and it's not without its costs. There were dashes to the restroom when I'd taken a big loss, and cocktail-fueled celebrations after work when I was on a roll. Stoic as I usually was on the outside, it took its toll on my insides, leaving me with a sensitive stomach. (Putting together Standard Oil wreaked such havoc on J.D. Rockefeller's digestive system that later in life he usually ate slices of bread dipped in milk, one of the few things that didn't upset his stomach.)

There are two types of traders: those who don't sleep when they're losing big and those who don't sleep when they're winning big. I was the latter. I'd be an excited insomniac when I was deep in the money, visions of sugarplums and big bonuses dancing through my head. Devastating losses were almost a sedative.

I had a nice middle-class upbringing, but my parents made it clear that once I completed my education, I had to fend for myself. Unlike most students today, I worked my way through college and graduate school and came out with very little debt. Of course, higher education is much more expensive now than it was back then, even after adjusting for inflation.

I was starting at zero, which is a lot better than starting in the hole. When you start at zero, you have to take risks if you're going to go anywhere. I took plenty of risks, realizing they wouldn't all pay off. Facing losses and failures, maybe I slept because I realized they were part of the game, the yin to risk's rewarding yang. They

29

never set me all the way back to zero, much less in the hole, and they were a necessary part of my education.

Don Corleone takes risks, makes mistakes, and learns from every one of them. The risk he will not take is displaying anger; the emotional outburst he detests the most. Even taking revenge, seemingly the birthright of every Sicilian male, "is a dish that tastes best when it is cold."

> *The Don considered a use of threats the most foolish kind of exposure; the unleashing of anger without forethought as the most dangerous indulgence. No one had ever heard the Don utter a naked threat, no one had ever seen him in an uncontrollable rage. It was unthinkable.*

—The Godfather

Virtually everyone in the novel and movies who gives in to his temper—Jack Woltz, Moe Greene, Frank Pentangeli, and Sonny—ends up the worse for it, usually dead.

Surely Michael Corleone had cause for anger when he was punched by the police captain, McCluskey. The blow knocked out teeth and shattered bones in his face. When a Corleone family lawyer asks Michael if he wants to press charges, Michael declines, mumbling in true *omerta* fashion that he slipped and fell.

> *At all costs he wanted to hide the delicious icy chilliness that controlled his brain, the surge of wintry cold hatred that pervaded his body. He wanted to give no warning*

to anyone in this world as to how he felt at this moment. As the Don would not.

—*The Godfather*

Indeed he wouldn't have.

There were other emotional displays Don Vito didn't like.

His life in a downward spiral, Johnny Fontane flies from California to New York to consult with his psychotherapist. He had left his children and faithful wife for a flagrantly unfaithful Hollywood slut. His voice shot, career fading, heath deteriorating, taking sleeping pills, and drinking too much, he whines to his Godfather. The Don's response is less than sympathetic.

"YOU CAN ACT LIKE A MAN!"
(The Godfather shakes Fontane and slaps him in the face.)
"What's a matter with you? Is this how you turned out, a Hollywood finocchio *that cries like a woman?"*
(The Godfather cries mockingly.)
"What can I do? What can I do?"

—*Part One*

Notwithstanding the Don's improper-speak towards women and gays (*finocchio* is Italian slang for homosexual), this was the shortest, cheapest, and most effective session in the history of psychotherapy. The tragi-comic scene marked the bottom for Fontane. With a little help from his Godfather, he got the movie part he wanted, won an Academy Award, resurrected his singing career, landed lucrative Las Vegas gigs, and became a powerful movie producer and Hollywood wheel.

How did the Godfather do it? He reminded Fontane of what it is *to be a man*. His godson had lived "like a fool" and had come to a "fool's end." You don't take a woman from a man more powerful than yourself, then expect that man to give you the leading role in his movie. You don't desert your wife and family for a tramp, no matter how beautiful. You don't let women dictate your actions, period. You don't let old friends down. Treat yourself with self-contempt and the rest of the world will follow. Act like a man and maintain your self-respect—the two are inseparable—and only then will you have any chance of successfully making your way in this world.

Ultimately, the Godfather was an advocate of reason—he could have been an Enlightenment philosopher. Throughout the novel, a man of respect must be a reasonable man, willing to listen to and reach agreements with other reasonable men. He believed that problems of business could always be solved among reasonable men. The reasonable man is serious, not given to frivolity or preoccupied with irrelevancies, in full control of his emotions. The Don detests unnecessary flourishes, even from buttoned-down *Consigliori* Hagen. Business should be kept strictly business.

Today, reason—our tool for grasping and adapting to reality—has been discarded in favor of emotions and wishful thinking. Notions of self-control are antique relics, consigned to an attic with other relics like civility and responsibility for one's own actions. All manner of foolishness is embraced as long as it feels good.

Reality is subjective and the truth is a matter of personal opinion. We can tax, spend, and borrow our way to prosperity. Perpetual war makes us perpetually safe. Innocents must be slaughtered in the name of religious and political causes. Boys are girls, girls are boys, men are women, and women are men if they feel like it. There are free lunches, along with free health care, college educations, housing, and whatever other "entitlement" a half-cocked politician, bureaucrat, academic, Hollywood star, or journalist dreams up. Productive people will happily turn themselves into slaves for the benefit of freeloaders. Wishing the woolly mammoth was slaughtered and dressed will make it so.

How can you have a shred of self-respect if you're unwilling to take care of yourself and demand that someone else do so? You are at the complete mercy of those who pay your way; they dictate your life, not you. No matter what they tell you about your "rights" to what they're giving you, they will have no respect for you or your "rights." The subjugated never get any respect, even when they scream for it at the top of their lungs. Nobody gets respect just because they demand it.

> *"It ain't the way I wanted it. I can handle things. I'm smart, not like everybody says, like dumb. I'm smart, and I want respect."*
>
> —*Part Two*

33

Fredo didn't get the respect he craved. Neither will pocket-stuffing politicians, paper-shuffling bureaucrats, generals who've lost every war they've ever fought, government-crony business people, safe-space students who graduate from their universities stupider than when they went it, media figures who wouldn't know the truth if it introduced itself on the street, degenerate celebrities, proper-speak and proper-think *pezzonovantis*, or all the other deluded fools, grifters, swindlers, and two-bit tyrants who've run this country into the ground.

Respect and self-respect, like everything in this life that makes it worth living, must be earned. Fredo sleeps with Tahoe's fishes. He got the respect he deserved.

Chapter 4

The Deadliest Sin

For some reason I don't recall, I was at home on a work day in the spring of 1991. That didn't mean I wasn't working. Trading municipal bonds back then was mostly via telephone.

I got a call from a trader with whom I did a lot of business. We had bought a large block of bonds together in what was called a joint account: we jointly owned the bonds and split the liability and risk. She was calling to tell me she had sold the bonds at a substantial profit. I was delighted and thanked her for running the account.

As I hung up the phone, I congratulated myself for my part in our astute purchase and sale. Damn, I was smart...brilliant! I had been at the partnership less than a year and was off to a great start.

Later that day, I got a call from one of my salesmen who covered large mutual funds. One of his funds had bonds for sale at a substantial discount to the rest of the market. I didn't know much about the bonds, but the salesman was convinced they were a good deal. There was the financial strength of the issuer, the city of Simi Valley, California, and the bonds had an additional backstop. The bond proceeds had been invested in a Guaranteed Investment Contract, or GIC, with an insurance company, Executive Life.

Not wanting to waste time and lose my shot at a good deal, I did no research on either the issuer or the insurance company. Brilliant traders don't need research! I told the salesman to buy a big slug of the bonds, which I figured I'd be able to resell at a large profit. I was on a roll!

Your worst trades follow your best trades.

The most insidious drug in the world is the cocktail of chemicals that surges through your system when you're on an ego high. Ego-juice is internally administered and you have no control over dosage. It's so damn pleasant you don't want to control it. The high can last anywhere from minutes to hours. It can be renewed any time you want, simply by recalling your triumph.

Executive Life had been one of Drexel Burnham Lambert's largest junk bond (bonds rated less than investment grade) customers. Executive Life's extensive portfolio of junk bonds backed up claims made against its insurance business, including its GICS. In the late 1980s a savings and loan scandal had knocked out a substantial source of demand for junk bonds and turned many savings and loans into forced sellers. Prices crumbled and Drexel went bankrupt in February 1990.

The mutual fund sold me the bonds at a discount because Executive Life's junk bonds were way underwater, posing a threat to the insurer's solvency. So much for not doing my homework. I owned the bonds for a couple of weeks, blissfully unaware, until someone mentioned to me that the market for Executive Life bonds was cratering. My stomach cratered with it.

I scrambled to get the Simi Valley bonds' indenture—the contract with bondholders that specifies the terms of the bond issue—and other official documents, and started doing the research I should have done before I bought the damn bonds. I discovered that Simi Valley could demand immediate repayment from Executive Life for the money it had tied up in the GIC. Bondholders representing a majority of the bonds had to make a demand on Simi Valley's city council for it to request repayment.

Eureka! I might be able to pull the fat from the fire. If Simi Valley got the money back it would redeem the bonds at full face value. I'd make a big profit on the bonds! I'd turn a bonehead mistake into another brilliant trade!

I drafted a letter to the Simi Valley city council making the demand and got a couple of mutual fund managers, who between them held a majority of the Simi Valley bonds, to sign it. In an emergency session, the Simi Valley city council voted to request the city's money back from Executive Life. The request was made the following day.

Simi Valley's bond issue was $15 million, a drop in the bucket for Executive Life, at the time California's largest insurance company. The bond indenture provision that allowed Simi Valley to demand repayment was unique to that bond issue; other bond issuers with Executive Life GICs didn't have that right.

Nevertheless, Insurance Commissioner John Garamendi, one of the biggest idiots ever to grace California state government (there's abundant competition) thought the request presaged the insurance company equivalent of a bank run with all of Executive Life's customers trying to immediately withdraw their funds.

Ten minutes of research or a couple of phone calls would have informed him that was not the case, but Garamendi panicked. He put Executive Life into conservatorship, which is like bankruptcy and stops all withdrawals from the company. Simi Valley couldn't get its money out and neither could anybody else. The value of Executive Life-backed bonds plummeted to around twenty cents on the dollar. Now I was looking at a loss of roughly 70 percent of my initial improvident investment. (Incidentally, Garamendi was a UC Berkeley and Harvard Business School graduate—don't be too impressed by gold-plated resumés. He's now a US representative from California.)

My boss, Don, was none too happy about the situation, but he didn't fire me. For over two years he and I, along with the firm's head of operations, endured long conference calls with attorneys as they detailed the legal and political machinations they were undertaking to get our money back. They did a good job and eventually our loss was reduced by about 75 percent. Executive Life was a source of controversy, scandal, and litigation for over twenty years. For all I know, there may still be lawsuits outstanding. It's one of the greatest travesties in the history of insurance.

I had to explain what happened and apologize to the partners on a conference call, not an easy thing to do. I didn't get much of a bonus the next few years.

Perhaps the most appropriate punishment would have been to write 10,000 times on a blackboard *Proverbs 16:18*.

Pride goeth before destruction, and an haughty spirit before a fall.

Not that it would have stopped pride or "an haughty spirit" on my part. Pride is the deadliest of the seven deadly sins because it recurs, regardless of past disasters and their calamitous consequences. There are some things people never learn, in spite of experience. Ego-juice is just that powerful.

People who come up the hard way don't usually forget where they came from, it helps keep them humble and hungry. Vito Corleone started with less than nothing—both his parents murdered, orphaned at a young age, sent to a foreign country with a new language and way of life—and he never forgot. A boast from the Don was as unthinkable as uncontrolled rage.

The Godfather's humility helped hold his empire together. Nothing will turn people against you quicker than displays of vanity, pride, and arrogance.

Don Corleone received everyone—rich and poor, powerful and humble—with an equal show of love. He slighted no one. That was his character.

—The Godfather

Among his acts of generosity, he funded the educations of poor but bright youths and lent money to those who couldn't obtain conventional credit. It was all done in a way that reflected his humanity. The recipients of his largesse were never made to feel that they were objects of charity, nor were there explicit reminders of an expected payback.

Not that there wasn't an expected payback. His beneficiaries were indebted to him, and many of them became successful in their own right. They were a bulwark of his empire, which he parlayed into the political influence that put in his pocket all those politicians and judges Virgil Sollozzo and Don Barzini coveted.

The children of self-made men are rarely made of the same stuff as their fathers. They come up the easy way, or at least easier than their fathers had it. Don Michael inspired fear, but not the affection, respect, and veneration that flowed to his father.

Michael's childhood was insulated by his father's wealth and power. Other than his father, the only person who stood as a challenge was his older brother Sonny; older brother Fredo was too weak. All the non-Corleone members of the Corleone family were deferential, he was the Don's son and potential heir to the business. Before turning killer, Michael looked like the all-American story, but Dartmouth and the military, even for a war hero, are not the same character-forging crucibles as Sicily's violent villages and New York's tenements.

We have *pezzonovantis* who rule absolute and supreme in their fiefdoms: executives, celebrities, professors, Popes, fund managers, generals, politicians, bureaucrats, winning coaches, and other exalted eminences. Don't expect humility from those who are never humbled. People insulated from question or challenge, their asses ceaselessly kissed, never criticized or condemned, and never considering any point of view but their own come to believe they're as great as they're told.

The absolute power secured by Michael's baptismal bloodbath worked its absolute corruption on his mind and soul. The contrasts to his father are telling. Unlike his father, Michael doesn't consult with his underlings and solicit their opinions, he issues orders.

In *Part Two*, Michael flies off the handle at Hagen for hesitating to give him the news about Kay's "miscarriage." Later, Hagen is upbraided for a job offer from outside the family that Hagen has already declined, and for questioning the planned murder of Hyman Roth. Michael goes out of his way to antagonize his adopted brother and Hagen protests.

> *"You gonna come along with me in these things I have to do or what? Because if not you can take your wife, your family, and your mistress, move 'em all to Las Vegas."*
> *"Why do you hurt me, Michael? I've always been loyal to you. What is this?"*

—Part Two

41

It's inconceivable that Don Vito would humiliate Hagen like that.

Michael's fury is at its most murderous when Kay tells him she's leaving him and that her miscarriage was actually an abortion. He goes off the rails, shouting at and slapping her. If Kay was anyone other than the mother of his children he would have had her killed.

Humans haven't evolved to the point where we can handle the kind of fortune, fame, and power modernity bestows upon the few. It's an open question if we ever will. Certainly Michael couldn't. For most of history, virtually everyone has lived in poverty and obscurity. There were the rulers and there was everybody else. More often than not the rulers were corrupt and tyrannical. Most everybody else stayed humble—their grinding circumstances gave them no basis for arrogance.

Making billions of dollars, acting in movies seen by millions, playing sports or concerts before stadiums packed with adoring fans, or presiding over a government that spends trillions of dollars and has the power to eradicate life on this planet produce addictive floods of ego-juice for which humans have no defenses. Our peasant ancestors at best got a few moments in the sun among a limited circle of family and friends. Even the rulers at the height of their pageantry and pomp received nothing like the attention, deference, and adulation in which some of our *pezzonovantis* bask.

We peasants still have our restorers of humility. Spouses, children, and friends serve up constant reminders of our fallibility and weaknesses, as do our jobs, coworkers, and bosses. We all fail occasionally, thank goodness. While the high and mighty don't have to deal with the consequences of their failures (everybody else does), we must deal with ours. One benefit of trading: markets regularly kick you in the teeth, making it harder for ego to run riot.

Most Americans are surprised to learn that much of the rest of the world despises them. It's not entirely fair, the rest of the world doesn't see most Americans. What they do see is Washington, the world capital of arrogance, blundering from one endless war to the next, browbeating and sanctioning anyone who won't get with its program.

> *"There are men in this world," he said, "who go about demanding to be killed. You must have noticed them. They quarrel in gambling games, they jump out of their automobiles in a rage if someone so much as scratches their fender, they humiliate and bully people whose capabilities they do not know. I have seen a man, a fool, deliberately infuriate a group of dangerous men, and he himself without any resources. These are people who wander through the world shouting 'Kill me. Kill me.' And there is always somebody ready to oblige them."*

—*The Godfather*

Don Vito wasn't talking about US foreign policy, but he could have been. For years we've gone looking for trouble in places like Vietnam and the Middle East, and we've found it. Hundreds of thousands of our own military and millions of people in other lands dead, trillions of dollars spent—much of it borrowed and not repaid—and nothing but woe to show for it. The US government vastly overestimates its own capabilities and underestimates those of its adversaries, wanders through the world wreaking havoc, and shouts its hypocritical nonsense, which sounds just like "Kill me! Kill me!" to the millions of enemies it makes. They're ready to oblige. That this will end in disaster is as assured as this evening's sunset.

Pride goeth before destruction, and an haughty spirit before a fall.

The greater the fool the greater the arrogance, which is why ship-of-fools Washington is the world capital. We've reached an apex of arrogance when the presidential candidate for a major political party calls a large swath of voters "deplorables." What's deplorable is that we even know Hillary Clinton's name. She owes it all to Bill, which is why she has stuck with him. On her own she doesn't have the smarts or political skill to get elected county clerk.

Americans who protest the unfairness of tarring an entire nation with the government brush protest too much. We've elected fools, we're coming to fools' ends, and the rest of the world knows it. In general, ordinary Americans don't make a good impression in foreign encounters. Listening and considering other people's points of view, especially foreigners', are not exactly national strengths.

Some years after my Executive Life fiasco, the trader with whom I had the successful joint account tried to hire me. I was interested. She was the head trader in the

Los Angeles office of a big Wall Street firm. The trading involved larger positions and was more sophisticated than what I was doing. I would make more money and there were reasonable prospects for advancement. The woman was the best municipal bond trader in California. I liked her and would learn from her. The business she did generated huge profits for her firm and for those with whom she did business. Consequently, she was also the most powerful trader in California.

Things were proceeding smoothly. I had gone to New York and been approved by the head of the municipal bond division. I was going with the trader to dinner, where we'd meet her boss and potentially seal the deal. As we drove along, she asked me, "Do you know what the best part of this job is?"

"No."

"Everybody kisses your ass."

I knew right then I wasn't going to work for her. To me, the only thing worse than kissing ass is having my ass kissed. If she thought having her ass kissed, rather than the job itself, was the best part of the job we weren't on the same page. And if she liked—and undoubtedly expected—to have her ass kissed, how long would it be before I would have to bend the knee? She would be my boss, after all.

At dinner I dreamed up some reason why I wasn't quite ready to shake hands on the deal. A few days later, my boss, Don, took me to lunch at his highbrow club. After Executive Life, I had made the firm a lot of money and he considered my department the best run in the firm. He knew I was talking with the other firm and didn't want to lose me. We had one of those pleasant "negotiations" where you get pretty much everything you ask for. Don and I shook hands and after lunch, I called the trader and turned down her offer.

I lost touch with her, but I think she wised up. Getting your ass kissed grows tiresome and you come to distrust and ultimately despise every kisser. Her firm was rife with internecine politics. A lot of people inside and outside the firm resented her success. She was off-the-charts bright and could not and would not suffer fools. She had plenty of money. When I found out she was leaving the bond business I wasn't surprised. I heard she volunteered at the school her two sons attended—nowhere near as remunerative, but certainly more rewarding.

Chapter 5

Have More Than Thou Showest

He claimed that there was no greater natural advantage in life than having an enemy overestimate your faults, unless it was to have a friend underestimate your virtues.

—*The Godfather*

The Corleone family is in decline. The Godfather has sued for peace in the Five Families War. At a meeting of the nation's Mafia dons, he agrees to use his political influence to protect the drug trade. It's the same deal he rejected from Virgil Sollozzo, which had precipitated the war. The Godfather foreswears vengeance for Sonny's murder—his natural right as Sonny's father—only warning that if something, anything, happens to Michael, then hiding in Sicily, he will blame some of the men in the bank conference room.

In the ensuing months, the Corleones' slide accelerates. The Godfather goes into semiretirement, entrusting the family business to Michael, an unknown quantity who doesn't command the respect his father does. The other New York families make inroads into Corleone territories and there is no retaliation. The family prepares to slink out of New York for Las Vegas's gambling and entertainment.

Matters come to a head at a meeting in the Godfather's library among the family's leadership—the Godfather, Michael, *Caporegimes* Clemenza and Tessio, *Consigliori* Tom Hagen, and Michael's brother-in-law Carlo Rizzi. Clemenza and Tessio complain about Barzini's incursions, but Michael won't give them permission to recruit new men and fight back. Capable and loyal Tom Hagen is demoted from *consigliori*, he'll be the family's lawyer in Las Vegas. Ominously, Michael announces that Carlo Rizzi will be his "right-hand man." Doesn't he realize Rizzi was behind Sonny's murder?

Clemenza protests to the Godfather and asks for permission to form his own family. Tessio pleads with him as well. The Godfather appeals to their loyalty to him and their faith in his judgment, and tells them to "be a friend to Michael and do as he says."

Michael blandly assures them that there are things being negotiated that will solve all their problems and answer all their questions. It's the Mafia equivalent of corporate-speak, the spokesperson assuring an anxious audience that the company's cash position is strong, its credit solid, and its finances in order the day before it files for bankruptcy. Michael even tells the *caporegimes* that they can form their own families after the move to Las Vegas. What could be weaker than the captain giving his crew permission to jump ship?

In Las Vegas, Moe Greene typifies the widespread contempt for the family, insulting Michael repeatedly. The Corleone family lacks muscle and is being chased out of New York, the Godfather is sick, Greene talks to Barzini, head of the rival family now considered the strongest in New York, and yes, Greene slapped Fredo around, but Fredo deserved it. As he leaves the room, Greene acerbically tells Michael he made his bones (his first murder) while Michael was still going out with cheerleaders.

Michael and the Godfather have the world exactly where they want it.

But now he was sure that in the subtle and complex mind of the Godfather a far-ranging plan of action was being initiated that made the day's happenings no more than a tactical retreat.

— The Godfather

It's a credit to Tom Hagen that he realizes right after the meeting of the dons that nothing is as it seems. The Godfather is already cooking up a plan, for which he has to have his exiled son back in the United States, legally safe, and in training to assume control of the empire. The retreat has to appear cowardly, a full-blown, unmanly exercise of terrible judgment. Michael's intelligence and strength have to be hidden, the Godfather's deterioration overstated. The Corleone family must meekly abide by the negotiated peace and not respond to the incursions and insults.

Hiding your side's true strength from your enemies and exaggerating your weaknesses is not exclusively a Corleone or Mafia tactic. Generations of military strategists have recommended it. The other side directs less firepower and troops against you and perhaps relaxes a bit or even gets overconfident.

There is another, more exclusively Mafia rationale for Michael and the Godfather's elaborate stratagem. The library meeting is a loyalty test. Will Tessio, Clemenza, and Hagen stick with the family despite its deteriorating position, or will one or more turn traitor? The Godfather believes there will be a betrayal, warning Michael that someone Michael absolutely trusts will set up a meeting with Barzini, guaranteeing Michael's safety. At the meeting, Michael will be assassinated.

"Barzini's dead. So is Phillip Tattaglia, Moe Greene, Stracci, Cuneo. Today I settled all family business, so don't tell me you're innocent, Carlo. Admit what you did."

—Part One

Not on Michael's above list, but soon to be dead are Tessio and Carlo himself. The Godfather and Michael's plan has worked—posthumously in the Godfather's case—and Michael is now indisputably the most powerful don in New York and the entire country. It couldn't have happened if the Corleones' enemies hadn't overestimated the family's faults, and if ostensible friend Tessio hadn't underestimated Michael's virtues, flushing himself out as the traitor.

There are probably fewer people who appreciate the benefits of being underestimated than who know that the title of this chapter—*Have More Than Thou Showest*— comes from Shakespeare's *King Lear*. It's the Fool's advice to the king.

> *Mark it, nuncle.*
> *Have more than thou showest,*
> *Speak less than thou knowest,*
> *Lend less than thou owest,*
> *Ride more than thou goest,*
> *Learn more than thou trowest,*
> *Set less than thou throwest,*
> *Leave thy drink and thy whore*
> *And keep in-a-door,*
> *And thou shalt have more*
> *Than two tens to a score*

Our age ignores that sound advice.

An appreciable portion of our gross national product is paid lying. Advertising, the media, public relations, propaganda, publicity, and politics are devoted to deception and to making people and products appear better than they are. There are celebrities whose sole claim to fame is that they're famous. Success supposedly demands that you impress people every step of the way. Self-promoters used to be known as braggarts and blowhards, now they get elected president.

Once upon a time, the first step in a business career was learning a business. Now it's getting a Masters of Business Administration, or MBA. As a holder of one of those diplomas, from the Haas School of Business at UC Berkeley, I can honestly say that it's the most useless degree this side of sociology, ethnic, racial, and gender studies, and the other proper-thought and proper-speak indoctrinations that litter college catalogues. Unlike those academic concentrations, an MBA may get you a job, so thoroughly has the corporate world brainwashed itself on its merit. However, if you really want to learn how to run a business there are far better options.

In an MBA program you'll learn accounting and statistics. They are the numerical languages of business, essential knowledge, but are available from books or online at a small fraction of the cost. You'll also learn the pet theories of your professors in finance, marketing, industrial organization, entrepreneurship and the other business sub-specialties. The old question—If you're so smart why aren't you rich?—applies in spades.

If I hadn't forgotten every theory of finance I learned at Berkeley I wouldn't have made a dime trading bonds. Cutting through all the business school theories, Wall Street analyses, and the media's after-the-fact rationales, financial markets are exercises in crowd psychology.

Speculators and investors who realize this differ on how to capitalize on it and how to measure crowd psychology, but if you follow Warren Buffett's advice— be fearful when others are greedy, and be greedy when others are fearful—in the long-term you'll do just fine as either a speculator or an investor. Buffett has practiced what he preaches, which together with a legendary ability to dope out businesses, their managements, and their financial statements has made him one of history's greatest investors, if not the greatest. He has an MBA, but I think he would have done just as well without it.

When I bought while everyone else was selling and sold when everyone else was buying, I generally made money. When I ran with the crowd in either direction, I most often lost it: I was a fool and came to a fool's end. Being a contrarian requires stubborn independence and thinking for yourself. Sometimes it doesn't work out, but over the long-term it's a simple and usually profitable strategy...and it requires no MBA.

What you mostly learn in business school is how to impress, to make yourself look better than you actually are. Most importantly, you learn how to interview—B-school is a high-class finishing school. At the priciest ones, prestigious corporations flock to offer the so-called best and brightest six-figure jobs. The people making the offers were once on the other end, receiving such offers, and so the cycle perpetuates itself: MBAs hiring MBAs. It also perpetuates the delusion that upon graduation graduates can run a business and it's appropriate that they do so.

B-school grads make dandy PowerPoint presentations. They pick up corporate-speak: *action item, benchmark, best practice, bring to the table, data point, empowerment strategy, impact* (as a verb) and *impactful* (ugh!), *modularity, moving forward, paradigm, reach out, teamwork, think outside the box, touchpoint, touch base,* and *zeitgeist,* among the many unmemorable words and phrases that comprise American business's stultifying, colorless jargon. For addressing the public, media, and government officials they employ proper-speak and either proper-thought (if they believe what they're saying), or rank hypocrisy (if they don't).

That's not to say that many of the hires don't go on to successful careers. They do, but that success has little to do with what was learned in business school; they would have been as successful without it. The requirement for an impressive credential acts as a gatekeeper to the corporate world. Like fraternity members who embrace the Hell Week rituals they hated as pledges, few who get an MBA challenge the system once they're part of it.

I worked at a variety of different jobs to pay for undergraduate and graduate schools. The summer after my first year in graduate school I was in Reno, where an uncle had found me a job in a casino. I also picked up a night job with a service that cleaned and maintained parking lots. The owner of the company wanted to retire. He offered to open up the books, put a fair price on the business, sell it to me, and finance my purchase.

At the time, I was too enamored of the MBA to take him up on it. Looking back, I would have done just fine if I had. Reno grew like a weed and there would have been plenty of opportunities to expand, not just in the parking lot business but into other businesses as well. I would have learned more about business than I did in B-school. Ultimately I might have made more money than I did as a bond trader.

The best business education is running a small business. Successful owners are jacks of all trades, incredibly resilient and resourceful. If you're contemplating B-school, consider taking part of the substantial money you're going to spend (and for which you may be going into debt), do your homework, and find a small business to buy.

If you can make money from a food wagon, an Internet startup, a carpet or house-cleaning franchise, or a landscaping service you probably have the chops and moxie to make it in almost any kind of business. You'll acquire a wealth of experience, have two years of positive rather than negative cash flow, and save and perhaps invest much of the money you would have spent on B-school. You may also find that you're the best boss you're ever going to have.

If you're absolutely certain that a gilded credential is essential to launching your business career, consider law school. You'll actually learn things that will help you in business. Sad to say, but whatever business you go into, you're going to run into the law and government. Even kids' lemonade stands need permits.

I went through the combined JD (*Juris Doctor*) and MBA program at UC Berkeley. I graduated from Boalt Hall Law School and passed the California Bar Exam. I never practiced law and I'm an inactive member of the California Bar Association. If I had to do it over again, I'd drop business school like a hot rock and keep law school—the training has been invaluable. How can knowledge of the laws of contracts, corporations, property, personal injury, securities, civil procedure, taxes, bankruptcy, antitrust, commerce, and secured land transactions not be worthwhile in a business career?

The Godfather recognized the value of legal training.

"Lawyers can steal more money with a briefcase than a thousand men with guns and masks."

—*The Godfather*

Many lawyers end up in business (some end up in organized crime), and not just in corporate counsel roles. I've often wondered why more non-legal businesses don't try to hire law students straight from law school.

In a business school finance class we were discussing the optimal mix of debt and equity financing for companies. It's a big issue, at least in B-schools, and papers and books have been written about it.

"Anybody here know what a debenture is?" I asked.

I got a lot of blank stares.

"A debenture is an unsecured corporate bond, backed by the general corporate credit and not specific assets." This I had learned in a corporate law class. "Am I the only one here who thinks it strange that in a class on corporate finance we learn all these theories on optimal financing arrangements, but nothing about different types of bonds?" The issue wasn't irrelevant. Different types of bonds pay different interest rates, which affect a corporation's financing costs.

I saw the fleeting grimaces that flash across people's faces when they're confronted by an uncomfortable idea. The microseconds between such ideas and forgetting about them is rivaled only by the infinitesimal time it takes husbands to forget what their wives just told them. The class quickly moved on to another discussion.

Not only do you learn more about business in law school than you would in B-school, but it improves your thinking, writing, and speaking skills. Many business people could stand improvement in all three.

Law school also offers superb training in separating business from personal. Lawyer Tom Hagen takes heaps of abuse from Jack Woltz and never loses his cool. Professors shred your arguments with a few questions—the Socratic method—and red-X entire pages of your legal briefs. You either develop a thick skin or law school is pure misery and you'll likely go into another line of work.

My training has paid for itself many times over. Recently I've been involved with a startup as both an investor and executive. The legal work I've done has saved thousands of dollars the company would have paid if it had hired outside lawyers. (It's news to Silicon Valley, but for most startups cash is scarce, and ours is no exception.)

So not everything I know about business I learned from *The Godfather*. I picked up a thing or two from law school, and a thing or two from business itself during my career. However, you can learn a lot more about business from *The Godfather* than at business school, and you'll save yourself a ton of dough. A 1969 hardcover first edition of *The Godfather* will run you less than an average trip to the grocery store. Two years at a top-ranked business school will cost you several thousand times more than that. To lapse into MBA-speak: the value proposition is obvious.

Without that MBA on your resumé, you stand a better chance of being underestimated. Although you may not be planning on murdering your enemies en masse to "assume and consolidate your nefarious power," (*Part*

Two) there are still advantages to being underestimated. Business is competition, and there's nothing wrong with your competitors overestimating your faults. It makes them cocky and complacent, which redounds to your advantage *if you stick to business.*

Have you ever happened upon a cafe or bistro you knew nothing about and had an enchanting meal? The food is superb, the service excellent. The place has an ambience and charm all its own, enhanced by the decor and lighting. Perhaps the chef emerges from the kitchen and greets you at your table. The other guests are relaxed and friendly. From the first sip of your cocktail to the last morsel of dessert, it's a perfect experience in every way. It may be the opening act of a memorable night with your dinner companion. You can't wait to share your discovery, but you have second thoughts. Popularity has ruined many a restaurant, or at least made it hard to get a reservation. Better to keep it a secret.

Many restaurants do wall-to-wall advertising and prosper, but their patrons don't think of them as cherished "discoveries." Similarly, many successful people do wall-to-wall advertising. They live in ostentatious mansions, drive flashy cars, have drop-dead gorgeous partners, get their kids into the best schools (by fair means or foul), employ high-priced personal trainers to sculpt their bodies, dress well, speak articulately, and are absolute masters of the first impression. There's no sense of discovery with such people, they simply overwhelm you.

Do you want to be like that? When I meet someone who's too good to be true, my immediate instinct is to start looking for contrary evidence. Having created that amazing first impression, what are the chances you can live up to it in the long run? Aren't you setting yourself up for disappointment among those you first impressed?

There are benefits to being an unknown quantity, benefits completely missed in our hype and hard-sell culture. The greatest natural advantage is having your enemies overestimate your faults, but another great natural advantage is having fools do so. Reveal yourself a little at a time and the fools who prize first impressions will underestimate you and fall away. The wise will gradually come to see and appreciate you for what you are.

Instead of worrying about the impression you're making on people, holding back allows *you to evaluate them*. It's a hallmark of honesty, confidence, competence, and strength, completely at odds with the contemporary mindset.

Humans have not evolved to the point where they can talk and listen at the same time. The likelihood of learning something is far higher with your mouth shut rather than open. *Speak less than thou knowest* and you can listen to what other people knowest, learn about them and what they're talking about, and understand their point of view. Asking questions clarifies and elicits still more useful information.

When they went into the house the Don said to Hagen, "Our driver, that man Lampone, keep an eye on him. He's a fellow worth something better I think." Hagen wondered at this remark. Lampone had not said a word all day, had not even glanced at the two men in the back seat. He had opened the door for the Don, the car had been in the front of the bank when they emerged, he had done everything correctly but no more than any well-trained chauffeur might do. Evidently the Don's eye had seen something he had not seen.

— *The Godfather*

The wise search for those who have more than they show and speak less than they know. The Don had seen someone who kept his mouth shut and his mind on the job. That says a lot to a man whose life and business depend on his ability to evaluate people about whom he has limited information. Refuse to play the "impress" game and you won't wow the crowd, but you may well attract the attention of someone who will end up mattering to you far more than the crowd. It's quality over quantity. By the end of *The Godfather*, Lampone is a *caporegime.*

When I was working at the Wall Street firm in Los Angeles, I got a call from Don, the majority owner and managing partner of the private partnership where I went to work. We had never met, but he was looking for a new head of the fixed income department. I never did learn how he discovered me, but the call initiated discussions that led to my hiring.

Don was quality, and didn't at all mind being underestimated, as I noted in my eulogy.

And then there was the defining feature of Don's personality — his probing, prodigious intellect. There are plenty of bright people out there, but it's rare to find a man of Don's candlepower, who obviously must recognize his own capabilities, but who has no need to have those capabilities recognized by anyone else. He was so confident of his own smarts that he was never afraid to ask what other people might think were "stupid" questions.

I know he was wealthy, having made many profitable investments in stocks, real estate, and businesses, well-educated, and extraordinarily intelligent. None of this did I learn from him (although there was no way he could hide his extraordinary intelligence). He was the antithesis of the need to impress. He drove a seven-year-old, bottom-of-the-line Lexus and flew coach. He was perhaps the best listener I've ever known—he wasn't asking all those questions for his health—and had a phenomenal ability to remember names. Under him the partnership was consistently profitable and the partners enjoyed a high return on their invested capital. I learned a lot from Don.

Now that I'm involved with a startup, I'm always looking for potential employees who have more than they show and speak less than they know. I've got my eye on one. We've been to lunch and he can't make small talk to save his life. He's usually quiet, although I've had hours-long conversations with him. He has few friends, but those few are friends for life. I doubt if the impression he makes on other people has ever crossed his mind. He's not arrogant or mean, in fact he's very kind, helping innumerable people in innumerable ways. But he prefers his own company and keeps to himself.

Why would I want to hire this guy who swims so far from the social mainstream? He's my brother, but that's irrelevant. Our startup is commercializing an innovative technology. One of its applications has to do with internal combustion engines. My brother is off-the-charts bright and knows everything there is to know about every kind of engine—he was a Ford mechanic and he now teaches auto and truck mechanics. Like most businesses these days, ours will make extensive use of computers and the Internet and he's a computer whiz. He can take apart or put together just about anything. His idea of a great weekend is to install a sprinkler system or build a storage shed. It'll take an attractive offer to get him, but his many talents and strengths would be a boon for our startup.

And he doesn't have an MBA.

Chapter 6

Bonds, Not Ties

As rich and powerful as the Godfather becomes, he never loses sight of the reciprocal strands of respect, obligation, honor, and loyalty due family, friends, fellow Sicilians, and the Catholic church. These are not ties that bind. They are bonds, sources of strength, foundational stones of his life and empire. Such bonds have bolstered the human race for most of its history. That they are now under sustained assault would strike Don Corleone as foolishness. Their proposed replacement would strike him as madness.

The family became the basic unit of human society not because men were a patriarchally oppressive conspiracy bent on enslaving their wives and children, but because it made the most sense. Humans reproduce, having filled the planet with almost eight billion of their kind. Women are vulnerable during pregnancy and when they're caring for infants and children. Men are physically stronger and better able to provide sustenance and protection. A division of labor suggests itself. Women stay home and care for the children while men hunt mammoths, farm, tame fire, invent the wheel, propitiate the gods, battle enemy tribes, and other exciting lines of work.

Although punctuated by the occasional catastrophic setback, the phenomenal increase in human population suggests this division of labor has been, from an evolutionary standpoint, quite successful. From that standpoint everyone gains. Children and grandchildren receive the care and training they need and perpetuate the genetic line. As they grow older and are able to work, they're an economic asset for their parents and grandparents. The extended family is the safety net, with younger family members caring for the elderly.

"Good, because a man who doesn't spend time with his family can never be a real man."

—Part One

In the Godfather's formulation, supporting a family—spending time with it; providing for a wife, children, and elderly members of the extended family; making the hard decisions; disciplining and training the children, and doing all the other unnoticed but necessary things fathers do—*makes a man a man.* Men with families labor for their daily bread, take risks, work to improve their situation, and otherwise engage in constructive pursuits, usually as much or more for their families as for themselves.

If a man who doesn't spend time with his family can never be a real man, do we have a term other than "miserable excuse for a man" for the worthless trash who father children but want no part of their upbringing? What can be more repugnant than spilling your sperm and taking no responsibility for the consequences? It destroys lives and dramatically reduces children's chances for success or happiness. Some of the groups who most loudly bewail their persecution have illegitimacy rates of 60 or 70 percent. They drape 100-pound millstones around their children's necks, wonder why the kids never win the race, and blame it on other, less-burdened competitors.

Won't a man who fails the tests of fatherhood and family also fail the tests of friendship? How can a father who has no loyalty to his children—his own blood—or their mother have any loyalty to his so-called friends? He'll abandon them at the first inconvenience, just as he did with his children and their mother.

When Bill Clinton was president it became fashionable to say that qualities of character a man demonstrates towards his family are irrelevant to his quality as a man. Restate that as: whether or not a man deliberately harms his own family has no bearing on whether or not that man will deliberately harm anyone else. If you want to buy into that proposition, be my guest, but do it with your own money.

A mother deludes herself if she thinks she can do as well bringing up her children by herself, or with help from relatives, revolving door boyfriends or girlfriends, the government, or the occasional appearance of the father as she could if the father is full-time committed to her and the family. The most masculine thing a man can do is accept responsibility for his family, but today's

Robert Gore

politics, divorced from reality as they are, deride and reject both family and masculinity.

In *The Godfather* novel and movies, individual interests are subordinated to the family, the sacred unit. Young Vito Corleone takes up a life of crime to feed his family. Going all in, Michael takes up a life of crime because the family is under attack. Connie must somehow "forget" that Michael has murdered her husband and reconcile with him and the family. There is no forgiveness involved because like God, family cannot be forgiven.

"I know it was you, Fredo. You broke my heart. You broke my heart."

—Part Two

Michael plants the kiss of death because Fredo has committed the most unforgivable sin in the Sicilian and Mafia firmament: he betrayed the family. Michael is so shocked he brooks usual Corleone protocol and lets a victim know that his transgression has been discovered and the victim is a dead man. Michael later observes another Corleone protocol—keeping his enemy close—and puts Fredo under Lake Tahoe house arrest until the time is right for retribution.

Murdering Fredo is not Michael's crossing-the-River-Styx moment it's sometimes made out to be. That canoe launched when Michael whispered to his father in the hospital room, "I'm with you now. I'm with you." At that moment he subordinated his conscience to the moral code of the Mafia. Under that code, there can be only one fate for a member like Fredo who betrays the family. Michael's father would have approved of the murder had he been alive.

Calling the entire Corleone organization—or any other large-scale Mafia operation—a family is propaganda. It's meant to evoke the same sentiments towards the Mafia family that members have towards their real families. It's akin to the nonsense dished out by corporations about their employee "associates" and "partners," "our team," and "our corporate family." The executives will lay off employees in a heartbeat to save a buck; employees will leave in a heartbeat if they find a better deal. Anyone who doesn't see through the nonsense is destined to a disappointing career.

"All our people are businessmen, their loyalty's based on that. One thing I learned from Pop was to try to think as people around you think. Now on that basis, anything's possible."

—*Part Two*

Any don foolish enough to believe that his underlings would sacrifice their own interests for those of the organization is not long for this world. Michael recognizes that like any business, the Corleone family runs on self-interest. Wisely, he tries to see things as those around him see them.

Friendship is another word that means something different inside the Mafia. There, friendships are mutually beneficial business and political relationships inside and outside the family. In *Part Two*, Senator Pat

Geary, indulging in his favorite perversions at a Corleone whorehouse, is drugged and the prostitute sordidly murdered. Geary awakens, confused and unable to remember the murder he didn't commit. He unties one of the bloody corpse's arms and tenderly places it by her side. Tom Hagen assures him the matter can be fixed; the prostitute has no family or friends and she'll be quickly forgotten. It will be as if nothing happened, and all that will remain is the senator's *friendship* with the Corleones.

Most business friendships aren't based on murder and implicit blackmail, but they are based on mutual benefit. The guy who said that if you want a friend in business get a dog wasn't too far from the mark. Stop benefitting a business friend, even one of long standing, and your friend will probably drift away. It's not what have you done for me lately, it's what can you do for me now.

When I was trading bonds, I had all sorts of friends. They made money off of me; I made money off of them. You can take all the sincerity on Wall Street, put it in a thimble and still have room for a good-sized thumb. I wasn't surprised when I received only a couple of calls after I got fired. Through the years I'm sure I didn't call people who had met with misfortune and who regarded me as a friend. Real friendship and loyalty are rare in business, and that's the way it has to be. The annals are filled with stories of failure where friendship and family were put before sound business judgment.

At a conference I attended, an executive claimed her poultry processing company befriended its chickens. Lighting, heating and all other living conditions were continuously adjusted to keep the birds happy, she gushed. Happier poultry may be better tasting poultry, but in the end they still kill the chickens. When business tells you it's your friend, that it cares for you and your happiness, keep those chickens in mind.

The government says it wants to be not just your friend but your family, cradle to grave. It provides anything for which enough people have clamored: maternity benefits, medical care, child care, education, food, housing, money, pensions, and death benefits. Cradle-bound children on college campuses howl for still more: free college and guaranteed jobs afterwards. They need their diapers changed, but eventually they'll probably get what they're crying for.

Just as Don Corleone wants something for the services he performs for his friends, the government wants something for what it provides. It steals from some, gives to others, keeps much for itself and its friends, but unlike a Mafia don, it wants your soul, regardless of where you fit in this scheme.

If you're one of the hard-working unfortunates from whom it takes, the government expects docile compliance. You might not like this state of affairs and the government will tolerate a bit of grumbling. However, any serious objection to its right to steal what you've earned will be dealt with harshly.

There are highly productive people who don't protest their own enslavement, they endorse it. Much of this is a con game. It helps make friends in the government, and to paraphrase Don Corleone, friends of the government, with lawyers and their briefcases, can steal more than a million men with guns. It's crony socialism:

you're raking in the government loot, so you're all for government.

A few wealthy people who receive nothing from the government except tax bills and regulatory hassles still proclaim their allegiance. Some of these people inherited their wealth or acquired it in enterprises that bestow outsize rewards on work of dubious merit—Hollywood, the recording industry, sports, fashion, art, publishing, the media, and academia. Deep down, many of them don't believe they deserve their wealth. They're almost relieved to have it taken from them and in today's political climate, pandering to government is the popular thing to do.

Many of the panderers claim that the government doesn't have enough money and should take more. Nothing stops *them* from sending in more, so we know their real object is to raise the tab for everyone else. They're angling for popularity, crony socialistic gravy, power, or—most likely—all three.

Every government bent on total control tries to suppress or eliminate competing loyalties, especially loyalties that go back centuries. Stepping in as the provider and letting fathers off the hook has been our government's main line of attack on the family. This has met with success, so it has turned its attention to other bonds.

The current fixation is eliminating the natural affinity most people have towards people who are like them, and the belief that their particular group is better than any other. The proper-speak *pezzonovantis*, commanding water to run uphill, try to prohibit racial and ethnic groups they don't like from touting their own group or disparaging others. All that does is drive such sentiments underground.

There is nothing underground about the Mafia of Don Corleone. It would drive proper-thought, proper-speak enforcers apoplectic, and the Corleone family would earn scads of demerits, fines, and public opprobrium. It unapologetically consists of males of Sicilian ancestry, with the occasional non-Sicilian Italian male thrown in. There are no women or members of historically disadvantaged minority groups. Improper-speak is rampant—Jews and blacks are routinely denigrated. The family's one attempt to reach out to an unrepresented ethnicity—making German-Irish Tom Hagen *consigliori*—is derided by the other families and reduces respect for the Godfather.

Don Vito's *consigliori* is anomalous, for the don certainly believes in the value of ethnic solidarity. Not only is it the glue cementing ties between families and friends, but Sicilians are steeped in the ways of the Mafia in the home country, particularly *omerta*, the law of silence. For men facing the prospect of imprisonment from the day they begin their careers, this assurance that their confederates and even their enemies will not rat them out to the authorities, regardless of the pressure brought to bear on them, is essential to their own keeping of the faith. The real life Mafia unraveled in the 1960s and 1970s when *omerta* broke down as successive generations' connections to Sicily and its traditions became ever more attenuated.

Erasing racial and ethnic loyalties has proved daunting for those governments that have tried. It has been impossible to eliminate religion, despite the best efforts of both intellectuals and governments.

There is a fable about the wind and the sun arguing about who can get a man to take off his coat. The wind goes first, blowing with all its might. The man clings more tightly to his coat. The sun beams brightly. The man gets hot and takes off his coat. The harder governments blow against religion, the tighter devoted adherents cling to it, even at the cost of their own lives. Religion strengthens them against depredation and tyranny, and inevitably outlasts the governments. Any government that wants to put a dent in religion should allow it complete freedom. Look at where Catholicism has gone in Europe and America.

The Corleones' fealty to the Catholic Church and its rituals may seem hypocritical. The Godfather's funeral launches the scheme to kill Michael and his counterattack. Michael renounces Satan at a baptism as his men shoot up his enemies. His son's first Communion is the backdrop for chintzy Lake Tahoe opulence, Connie's moral and spiritual deterioration, and corrupt political dealings. Michael seemingly reconciles with Fredo as their mother lies in her casket, but he's only moving his enemy that much closer.

Yet, along with family, friends, and Sicilian ethnicity, Catholicism is the glue holding the Mafia together. Their lives are exercises in hypocrisy, but they are all part of the same hypocrisy and observe the same rituals, hypocritical though that may be.

It was at this time that the Don got the idea he ran his world far better than his enemies ran the greater world which continually obstructed his path.

—*The Godfather*

The Godfather inarguably ran his world far better than governments, which have made a complete botch of it. He marshaled affinities and loyalties that have stood the test of countless centuries. That the *pezzonovantis* think they can suppress or destroy such bonds and replace them with mankind's falsest god—government—only demonstrates their stupidity and their corruption.

Chapter 7

Hollywood

From *The Godfather*, it's obvious Mario Puzo didn't like Hollywood. That antipathy ran through the novel, but was left out of the movies. Hollywood satirizes, criticizes, or scandalizes virtually every activity and endeavor...except Hollywood.

When he wrote the novel, Puzo had as much experience with Hollywood as he did with the Mafia—very little. Writing in the 1960s when the public was still enchanted by its glitz and glamour, he shows a seamier side. As with most institutions, Hollywood's standing has plummeted the last fifty years. Puzo's depiction is far less shocking now than it was then, it could have been based on current headlines.

Margot Ashton is one of Hollywood's marquee products, a movie idol, breathtaking beauty, and fantasy fixation.

On the screen her beauty was magnified, spiritualized. A hundred million men all over the world were in love

with the face of Margot Ashton. And paid to see it on the screen.
"Where the hell were you?" Johnny Fontane asked.
"Out fucking," she said.

—The Godfather

So much for unattainable. That's the reader's page three ice-water plunge into Hollywood. Two words in a sordid scene and the mystique shatters like the sugar-glass bottles they bust over heads in movie bar fights. A hundred million men's fantasy is just a better-looking grade of trailer-park trash. Her singing superstar husband is a besotted, jealous cuckold who can't even beat her up as she mocks him.

Fontane, Puzo's nod to Frank Sinatra (which Old Blue Eyes hated), rises from that humiliation, the nadir of his career, all the way back to the top. He plays a much bigger role in the novel than he did in *Part One*. Although he's smart, tough, and talented, there's little that's admirable about him or his comeback. When he throws himself on the mercy of his Godfather, he is, like most stars, a brat spoiled by success. He had everything, was losing it, and wants his Don to make it all better.

Like alcoholics, spoiled brats need their enablers to quit enabling and allow them to bear the consequences of their own actions. The Godfather is an enabler, he won't cut Fontane adrift. His godson stole a budding starlet from a powerful studio head, who understandably won't give Fontane the leading part he wants. No problem—what Johnny wants, Johnny gets.

Jack Woltz, the studio chief, discovers the head of his prize race horse, Khartoum (the British general, Charles Gordon, was beheaded during the siege of Khartoum in 1885), at the foot of his bed and shortly thereafter Fontane gets his movie role. Woltz had understood that a refusal to play ball might lead to trouble. However, he's out of his league when it comes to Don Corleone's audacious brutality.

What kind of man could destroy an animal worth six hundred thousand dollars? Without a word of warning. Without any negotiation to have the act, its order, countermanded. The ruthlessness, the sheer disregard for any values, implied a man who considered himself completely his own law, even his own God.

—*The Godfather*

When the novel was published, the notion that Hollywood and the Mafia could be in bed together was scandalous. Here again Puzo shines a light. It's clear from the failed negotiations between Woltz and Tom Hagen that the Mafia and the movie industry make common cause. Hagen offers to dry up a Woltz leading man's supply of heroin and eliminate impending labor problems. Later, the Godfather swings the Best Actor Oscar to Fontane through his influence in Hollywood's unions.

Woltz, like Fontane, is not an admirable man. They're two scorpions in a bottle and there would be few tears if they stung each other to death. However, egotistical, petty, and abrasive as Woltz is, it's his studio and his racehorse, and his property rights in both are heedlessly trampled.

The novel casts him in a far harsher light than the movie. *Part One* leaves out Woltz's predilection for young girls. He's not just rough-and-tumble Hollywood obnoxious, he capitalizes on the ruthless ambition of a harpy stage mother to molest her beautiful twelve-year-old daughter.

Tom Hagen witnesses the girl and her mother as they emerge from Woltz's mansion to a waiting limousine. The girl's mouth is smeared, her eyes are filmed over, she totters unsteadily as she tries to walk, and the harpy hisses at her.

The girl and her mother had made the trip with the movie producer. That had given Woltz enough time to relax before dinner and do the job on the little kid. And Johnny wanted to live in this world? Good luck to him, and good luck to Woltz.

—*The Godfather*

Once innocence is shattered it never gets put back together again. The young girl may get the stardom her mother craves, but she'll never escape the nightmares and psychological repercussions.

Inclusion of this scene in the movie would have diminished whatever sympathy the audience had for Woltz, but child molestation was taboo back then. It would have proved problematic for Hollywood's obsessive image promotion. Knowing what we know

now, it may have hit too close to home for some of the industry's *pezzonovantis*.

There's a certain irony that Hagen, *consigliori* and accomplice to a don guilty of a long list of capital crimes, finds Woltz and his world reprehensible. That world is not just harmless tinsel, it's a soulless, evil void masquerading as a glittering paradise. More evil than the Mafia? Perhaps.

Living in West Los Angeles, I ran into a few movie celebrities. In the mid-1990s, an actress lived down the street from me. She was from a movie family and had starred in one blockbuster. Her career faltered from there. I walked my dog every afternoon. Sometimes she'd be walking hers and we'd walk together.

She was pretty and a nice enough person, but not a scintillating conversationalist. One day the talk turned to politics. President Clinton had just signed a training and jobs bill.

"Isn't it wonderful!" she chirped. "This program will give disadvantaged young people self-esteem!"

Anybody who thinks the government can give someone self-esteem is dumber than a pet rock. If it could, the largest, most intrusive government in history would preside over the most well-adjusted population in history. I don't think that's the case.

On the debate team in high school and in classes and moot court in law school, I found the hardest arguments to address were those that came from left field. They're not germane to the topic under discussion, and invariably issue from someone who's not very bright. What the hell do you say to non sequiturs—announced in a triumphant tone that heralds a nugget of brilliance and conclusive proof that whatever you've said is wrong—that completely miss your point? I had the same perplexed, slightly stunned feeling about the self-esteem statement. What the hell do you say?

I forget what I said, or mumbled—something weak I'm sure. I should have just asked her how the government gives people self-esteem and let her blunder through an answer. The rest of the walk was mostly in silence.

Read celebrity press releases, always written by someone else, or listen to their public statements, mostly memorized lines written by someone else, and it's clear they're not the sharpest tools in the shed. You have to hear their spontaneous, unscripted utterances to realize how vacuous and stupid some of them really are. I resolved from then on to walk my dog at a different time of the day, and to steer clear of movie stars. For the most part I was successful.

One day I was sitting in a local deli with my son. A gentleman walked in who stood out from the holes-in-their-blue-jeans movie crowd—he looked distinguished. He was older and wore a dress shirt and slacks with a blue blazer. He also looked familiar. As he sat in the table next to ours I said, "I've seen you somewhere before."

"I'm Jon Voight, the actor."

So I had seen him on movie and TV screens. We talked about his films and acting. He was intelligent and inquisitive, asking me what I did and about my son. I asked if he had any children. He gave me a weird look and replied that he had two children.

Afterwards, I told a friend who lived across the street about the encounter. When I mentioned that I had asked

Voight about his children, she looked at me in amazement and said, "You don't know?"

"Know what?"

"His daughter is Angelina Jolie."

I never should have let my subscription to *People* magazine lapse. I may have been the only person in celebrity-obsessed West Los Angeles who didn't know about that father-daughter connection, especially since they had a spat that made headlines, but it shows how successful I had been at ignoring the movie crowd.

In *The Godfather*, the Don sets up Fontane as a movie producer, arranging financing for his favorite godson's first three pictures. Fontane calls an author whose book had been made into a movie, and whose latest book has movie potential. Puzo turns the author's story into a vignette about the way Hollywood treats writers.

After the author had signed his movie contract, he had gone to Hollywood expecting to be treated like a "wheel," but instead, "like most authors, had been treated like shit." The author went to dinner with a beautiful starlet, who deserted him for a "ratty-looking movie comic."

That had given the writer the right slant on just who was who in the Hollywood pecking order.

—The Godfather

Writers are like football's linemen—essential but under-appreciated. The money is good. I knew a writer for a top-rated comedy series and she lived in a gated enclave where Shaquille O'Neal and Kobe Bryant had lived. However, writers should get more respect than they do, they're the foundation for everything the entertainment industry does. Movies, TV series, and plays are only as good as their stories, and who creates the stories?

Good writing doesn't guarantee a good movie, but bad writing guarantees a bad one, which even a top-notch producer and director and a megastar cast usually can't save. Look at the careers of the big names in Hollywood and they all have their movies they'd rather forget, and hope everyone else does too. Bad writing is often the culprit.

I had my own near-brush with Hollywood as a writer. In the 1990s, working mostly on weekends I wrote my first novel, *The Gordian Knot*. It took about ten years to research, write, and edit. I was in a creative writing class and the woman who taught it liked my book. She invited me into her weekly writing group and after I had completed the book, offered to be my agent.

She called her contacts in the publishing industry, but there were no takers. Internet self-publishing was in its infancy and I self-published. That gave people like me a way around the publishing *pezzonovantis.* However, a multitude of writers were and are looking for a way around the *pezzonovantis*. Thousands of books are self-published and it's hard to get noticed. You not only have to have a good story, you have to have the time, energy, and aptitude for extensive self-promotion, not my forte.

I had a good story, but I didn't sell many books, in part because *The Gordian Knot* had its deficiencies aside from my self-promotional inadequacies. It was my first effort and although I learned a lot writing it, I still had a long way to go. The choice of title was unfortunate. Stick *Gordian Knot* in an Amazon search and you'll come up with at least twenty different listings. Never use a popular expression or cliché in a title if you want to sell on Amazon.

The story would have worked as a movie, and my agent tried Hollywood, where she knew some people. Again we struck out. I joined the several million people in Los Angeles who have failed to sell their movie ideas to the studios. The best thing about my first book was that I learned how to write a novel. My second one was better.

Among the scads of books and screenplays submitted to Hollywood, the law of averages says that some of them would make good movies. Paradoxically, the supply exceeds the demand as Hollywood slides into creative bankruptcy. By most measures other than box office receipts, which are inflated by ever-rising ticket prices, the big-screen movie business is—charitably—in a rut, and not so charitably going downhill.

They don't make 'em like *Part One* and *Part Two* anymore, and they haven't for some time. People forget that Paramount Pictures thought they were taking a huge risk making *Part One* and kept it low-budget. The dollars-and-cents people have always had their say in Hollywood, but now they hold complete sway.

Which is why the big production and promotion budgets are reserved almost exclusively for comic-book movies, sequels, and prequels, collectively known as franchises. I was bored with explosions, chase scenes, computer-generated special effects, and battles to the death long ago, but they'll keep milking the franchises until they run dry. If they were trying to turn *The Godfather* into a franchise with *Part Three* it didn't work. The majority of *Godfather* aficionados share my opinion that the movie should not have been made.

Good films still get produced, but mostly by independents on low budgets. Once in a while they break out, but usually they're confined to film festivals and limited distribution in large cities. Whatever the creative merits or flaws of movies that have won the best picture Oscar the last few years, their box office numbers indicate that relatively few people watched them.

Hollywood is isolated and insular, making it nearly impossible for people who are paid millions of dollars, live in posh enclaves, have their groceries purchased and food prepared for them, and are fawned on nonstop by their fans, toadies, and the media to identify with or understand the concerns and aspirations of those who are not so favored.

City slickers sometimes buy farms or ranches and think they can do better than the locals, although they've never stepped in cow shit and haven't a clue about growing crops or raising animals. Hollywood never steps in the cow shit that's part and parcel of daily life for the rest of us, and it hasn't a clue about how we live. If it makes a movie that strikes a responsive chord among us common clay, *it's by accident*

Actors' fates are tied to movie executives, audiences and the media liking them, thus acting, like politics, draws people who have a desperately neurotic need to be liked. In old Hollywood, studios limited their stars' public, unscripted appearances to preserve their biggest assets' mystique. It was a wise policy. Today, stars' foibles, perversions, and crimes are splashed across grocery store tabloids, the mainstream media, and the Internet.

Familiarity has bred contempt. The glamour is gone. Stand for nothing but your own fame and fortune and you'll end up as less than nothing. If you'll do anything to get what you want, you'll have no moral commitment to anything of value. Nature abhors a vacuum, and Hollywood's moral vacuum is filled with drugs, debauchery, scandal, and crime.

As a preemptive publicity screen and a salve for the quiet voice of conscience that can never be completely stilled, most stars adopt one or more causes. Africa seems to be a particularly fashionable fixation. Promote your solutions to the problems of that continent, directing cameras, media attention, and your conscience away from your depredations in Beverly Hills, Miami, Manhattan, London, and other celebrity playpens.

The glitterati adopt another moral balm: collectivist politics. Stealing and spending other people's money for your causes and beneficiaries is more virtuous than spending your own. Anyone who resists such theft is immoral. These are simple formulations; the only kind the stars can understand. Within their own crowd they confer admiration without accomplishment. Everyone else gets cloying righteousness, self-satisfied superiority, and sneering contempt towards the great unwashed.

Hollywood and Washington are joined at the hip. Their collectivist hive mind justifies the government's claim on all income and wealth. Politicians stream to the West Coast for fund raisers and publicity. Intelligence agencies, the military, and other government agencies help write scripts, provide technical assistance, and allow filming at their facilities. Hollywood promotes proper-speak and proper-thought. Stars are invited to Washington to testify before august bodies on the world's pressing problems. That they bring no expertise or intelligence to such problems bothers no one. Some of them go into politics.

The powerful and beautiful exempt themselves from the legal and regulatory garbage they heap on everyone else. That nauseating hypocrisy has greased Hollywood's long slide. Who wants lessons on virtue and wisdom from debauched fools? Who cares about their passionately promoted causes, well-publicized good deeds, and pious pronouncements? Who's going to pay their hard-earned money to see movies from a town and industry that hate them?

One character in *The Godfather*, absent from the movies, looked into the Hollywood abyss, saw it for what it was...and fell in: Nino Valenti. Nino was Johnny Fontane's buddy in New York and they sang together. Fontane went on to fame and fortune in Hollywood while Valenti drove a truck back home. When Don Corleone sets Fontane up as a movie producer, the unspoken test Fontane has to pass is to somehow take care of his old friend. He figures it out and invites Nino out to Hollywood.

Fontane takes him to a studio party, a private movie screening that's an orgy for past-their-prime women stars and Hollywood's young studs. When the lights go out, screen legend Deanna Dunn gives Nino a blow job. Afterwards, Fontane asks him if he had a good time.

Nino grinned. "I don't know. It's different. Now when I go back to the old neighborhood I can say Deanna Dunn had me."

Johnny laughed. "She can be better than that if she invites you home with her. Did she?"

Nino shook his head. "I got too interested in the movie," he said. But this time Johnny didn't laugh.

"Get serious, kid," he said. "A dame like that can do you a lot of good. And you used to boff anything. Man, sometimes I still get nightmares when I remember those ugly broads you used to bang."

Nino waved his glass drunkenly and said very loud, "Yeah, they were ugly but they were women.*"*

—The Godfather

This is Nino's introduction to Hollywood's "glamour" and he's not buying it, but he doesn't have the fortitude to head back to New York. He makes records and movies, becoming a star in his own right, all the while drinking himself to death. We'll leave Nino with the last word on Hollywood.

Michael was shocked at how Nino looked. The man was visibly disintegrating. The eyes were dazed, the mouth loose, all the muscles of his face slack. Michael sat on his bedside and said, "Nino, it's good to catch up with you. The Don always asks about you."

Nino grinned. "Tell him I'm dying. Tell him show business is more dangerous than the olive oil business."

—The Godfather

Chapter 8

Women

It was while this was going on that Michael was hit with what the Sicilians call "the thunderbolt."

***

This was an overwhelming desire for possession, this was an inerasible printing of the girl's face on his brain and he knew she would haunt his memory every day of his life if he did not possess her. His life had become simplified, focused on one point, everything else was unworthy of even a moment's attention.

—*The Godfather*

The woman who played Apollonia in *Part One*, Simonetta Stefanelli, could indeed evoke the thunderbolt. It is the best and worst thing that could happen to Michael. His passion for her is exquisite torture, beyond mere lust or love. It's an insatiable desire for her beauty, youth, and innocence, and a primal, not-to-be-reasoned-with imperative for ownership. He has to have her, and his icy self-control affords him no protection from his obsession.

He understood for the first time the classical jealousy of the Italian male. He was at that moment ready to kill anyone who touched this girl, who tried to claim her, take her away from him.

—*The Godfather*

Jealousy isn't exclusive to Italian males. The thunderbolt may be a Puzo literary creation, but even if it's just a hyperbolic extreme, any man who has loved a woman and lost her favor to another has known jealousy's tormented fury. Joy turns to rage in an instant. They're the hard-wired, inseparable yin and yang of love. Regardless of how well a man outwardly handles real or imagined infidelity by the woman he regards as his, even pretending it doesn't bother him, on the inside he's churning. We are all Othello.

That night and the weeks that followed, Michael Corleone came to understand the premium put on virginity by socially primitive people.

—*The Godfather*

That premium is closely related to jealousy. While men are jealous of current threats to the affection of their woman, they may be even more perturbed by past lovers. That's not confined to "socially primitive people." Thomas Hardy's *Tess of the d'Urbervilles* explores the premium put on virginity in late Victorian and hardly primitive England. It's been the norm from cavemen days and across geography and cultures.

When the cavemen were out hunting for mammoths, they couldn't divert mental and emotional energy worrying that their women were fooling around with somebody else. Insisting on sexual exclusivity wasn't just a psychological foible.

The biological and evolutionary bases for love and lust are straightforward—they lead to procreation. The emotional attachment of a father to his own children is usually not as strong as the mother's, but it's far stronger than the one he would have for another man's child by his mate. It's an unrelated mouth to feed from scarce food stores. Support in such instances entails self-sacrifice for a child with no genetic ties, an investment with no evolutionary return. Insisting on virginity and sexual exclusivity from his mate, backed by jealousy's power and threat of violence, raises the probability that he will be caring for the fruit of his own loins.

That the human population has multiplied many times over since cavemen days suggests that like the family unit, men's essential biological and psychological drives, primitive though they may be, have served their evolutionary purposes well. Now they're under both technological and ideological attack across much of the Western world.

The Godfather is almost wholly masculine. In the movies, there are one-and-a-half significant women's roles: Kay Adams and Connie Corleone. Apollonia is blown up 26 minutes after she first appears and both young and old Mama Corleones are bit parts.

The novel has a subplot featuring Sonny's wedding-day paramour, Lucy Mancini. After Sonny is killed, she moves to Las Vegas and eventually becomes engaged to a doctor, Jules Segal. This subplot is a diversion and serves little purpose, which was probably why it was omitted from the movies. It may be in the novel to give Puzo a soapbox on abortion.

Mafia wives were expected to have and raise children, cook, do the household chores, and keep themselves separate from their husbands' careers. Wives knew they were married to criminals, but questions were forbidden, fidelity was required, and they were to stick to their domestic duties and women friends.

The church quieted any qualms about the lives they were leading. They could pray for the souls of their husbands, as Kay, a newly converted Catholic, did at the end of the novel. A scene of her doing so was filmed as the finale but dropped from *Part One*. It should have been left in, a commentary on the malleability of belief.

Domestic duties and fealty to family became problematic for Connie after Michael murders her husband. She throws a venomous, hysterical tantrum, confronting Michael and Kay with his crimes. That's the last we see of Connie in the novel and *Part One*. She's swims in a toxic emotional pool as *Part Two* opens: flipping husbands, neglecting her children, and bitter towards Michael but dependent on him for money. Later, she repents.

"I think I did things to myself to hurt myself so you'd know I could hurt you. You were just being strong for all of us the way Papa was, and I forgive you...You need me Michael, I want to take care of you now."

—*Part Two*

In her new incarnation she wears severe black, but it might as well be sackcloth and ashes. She's submitted to the family and Michael. Now she's going to be his caring sister, surrogate mother and surrogate wife all in one. Michael needs her about as much as he needs a Senate subpoena. She undoubtedly makes delicious pasta, but she's essentially wiped herself out of existence—no job, no man, no spark, enough money to live on but not much of a life at the sterile Lake Tahoe compound. Perhaps she sees her children once in a while.

Unique among *Godfather* characters—aside from grandstanding politicians in *Part Two*—Kay finds the Mafia way of life morally objectionable. In the novel, after Michael returns from Sicily, he and Kay discuss his criminality.

"You're telling me you're a gangster, isn't that it? You're telling me that you're responsible for people being killed and other sundry crimes related to murder. And that I'm not ever to ask about that part of your life, not even to think about it."

—*The Godfather*

That's exactly what he's telling her, which was fine with the Sicilian peasant, Apollonia, but not an educated, 1940s American woman. Michael rationalizes that he must do what he must do for the family, and assures her the family will be legitimate in five years. He and Kay, "will be part of some country-club crowd, the good simple life of well-to-do Americans." They'll probably vote Republican. "How does that strike you for a proposition?" he asks.

Trade her conscience for the good life—it's an offer she should refuse. The way Michael has framed his offer alerts her to something else.

> *"How can you want to marry me, how can you hint that you love me, you never say the word but you just now said you loved your father, you never said you loved me, how could you if you distrust me so much you can't tell me about the most important things in your life?"*

> —*The Godfather*

He doesn't really love her, not deep down. His is a practical appeal for Kay to join a partnership for the perpetuation of the dynasty, dressed as a marriage. There is none of the passion that sent his heart racing when he first saw Apollonia, that kept him up night after night making love to her when they were married. Passion is not the foundation for many marriages, whether anybody admits it or not. However, Michael doesn't even tell Kay he loves her after she reminds him that he hasn't. His offer is made out of calculation, not can't-live-without-you desire and love.

Kay knows what she's getting into. For love, marriage, children and a comfortable lifestyle she stifles her doubts and conscience, but for how long? *Part Two*'s divorce is almost preordained, probably inevitable after Kay is almost killed in the bedroom ambush. Surrendering your soul is one thing, surrendering your life another. With a perfect subzero stare, Diane Keaton convey Kay's hostility towards and emotional distance from Michael as the family huddles in the living room after the shooting.

Kay is not what we would call a modern woman. Her career is teaching, one of the few acceptable for women at that time. Despite misgivings, she gives it up for the life of a Mafia wife.

Much has changed. Among a large swath of the female population, foregoing a career for marriage, family, and children is unacceptable. Males' former dominance of business, politics, and other professions and pursuits has been cast as patriarchal oppression that must be remedied. Masculine qualities and characteristics are in disrepute.

As for the overwhelming instinctual desire that drove Michael's obsession for Apollonia's youth, beauty, and virginal innocence, it's simply taboo. Any passion, and certainly lust, are suspect male snares that keep women from their true destinies as investment bankers, arc welders, lawyers, politicians, gunnery sergeants, software programmers, and the like.

For better or worse, women have joined the mammoth hunt. Contraceptives and abortion have freed them from pregnancy and child care; they don't have to stay in the cave. Laws have changed, customs, prejudices, and practices are changing, and women are increasingly represented in every field of endeavor, even the military. Many of them are just as good or better at their chosen occupations than men.

When I got into bond trading in the mid-1980s there were few women and they had to have six-inch-thick hides to put up with the garbage men dished at them. Although they were on their way out, hookers and strippers were still part of bond outings. By the time I left, women were commonplace and men— "encouraged" by the proper-speak and proper-thought proctors every securities firm installed—had learned to accept them, say the right things, and confine expressions of their true feelings to their buddies in the locker room.

While many jobs have their rewarding aspects, jobs are still jobs—work. Anyone who undertakes a career expecting fulfillment and Nirvana is liable to be disappointed. At best, you're interested in what you do and you don't mind working hard at it. However, there are no jobs that don't have their distasteful and tedious aspects. If you're lucky the more enjoyable parts make the less enjoyable ones tolerable, but what matters is whether the mammoth has been killed, not the personalities, egos, or emotional "needs" of the hunters.

The perfect-world builders are trying to build the perfect world, but until they do women who pursue careers must separate reality from ideology. Much as women may want to be judged on objective standards of merit, men are still men. Pass laws, propagate proper-speak, indoctrinate, install proctors, send men to reeducation camp...and biology still wins, there's no escaping testosterone. The guy in the indoctrination seminar likes the teacher's tits; the inmate in the reeducation camp can't keep his eyes off the warden's ass. All trying to negate biology has done is drive it underground; men are more surreptitious but no less salacious.

Women should also realize that men act differently around women than they do in exclusively male settings. A woman walking into a meeting with a group of men changes the dynamics. Women command awareness and attention, even if they think they're being ignored. Insecure males will play up to her or put her down—excessive deference or outright condescension. There may be sexual tensions and even rivalry among the males.

Men have been working with and competing against each other for so long that the rituals, expectations, communications, and behaviors are almost innate. Most men are more comfortable with other men than they are with women. The rules, explicit and implicit, are understood and accepted, having been inculcated since boyhood on playgrounds, athletic fields, and other male venues. Women upend the male applecart not just because men aren't used to working with them, but because they don't know the rules of the male game and so can't play by them.

Which brings up good old boys' clubs. Some of them are indeed bent on subjugating females. (Islam may be the ultimate good old boys' club.) However, good old boys' clubs are also an obstacle for talented, competent men who don't want to be one of the boys.

I was never a joiner. I stayed away from fraternities and clubs in college and graduate school. When it was time to find a job, the municipal bond business was a good old boys' club, the essential entrance requirement a stout liver. Job openings were filled by drinking buddies and relatives. I didn't belong. Fortunately, a banker setting up a new municipal bond department with no connections or experience in the bond business hired me as a trading trainee. He liked my resumé and the way I interviewed. Imagine that.

Similarly, my second job, in Los Angeles, came from a New Yorker with a New York firm, an outsider. I had been looking for a job in Los Angeles and had already been turned down by some of its good old boys, who then hired relatives and drinking buddies. The New Yorker was looking for smart people and had heard good things about my trading. He was an excellent boss, and when he left a few years later I was promoted to his job, head of the West Coast region.

The good old boys running the New York office got the bright idea to install an internal computer system with a screen that showed minute-by-minute how much money each region and trader was making. I was making more trading profits than everyone except a couple of New York traders with much bigger trading lines. Most of the bonus pool stayed in New York to take care of the good old boys, regardless of performance. I was being paid much less than less-profitable traders

Ideally killing mammoths should be about killing mammoths. The person who has the most to do with the kill should get the prime rib. Life and business are not always fair. Good old boys' clubs, and now good old girls' clubs, opposed to ideas and innovations from outsiders—or refusing to pay them what they're worth—can ruin a business in short order. American business is rife with such clubs.

If you're killing the mammoths and getting mammoth-burger instead of prime rib, start looking around. That's what I did with the New York firm, eventually landing at the private partnership. A few years later the New York firm, founded in 1879, ran into legal troubles and was acquired by a bank that merged it into its own operations. An illustrious name in finance was no more.

You're never going to keep business and personal completely separate in the workplace. Better companies do a better job of it, but the irrelevant always enters the mix. Historically, leaders of men have been disproportionately taller than average. Studies show that good looking members of both sexes are better rewarded than their equally accomplished but plainer peers. The gregarious tend to go farther than the introverted. People favor their own sex, race, and ethnic group when they hire and promote. It's not fair or right, but it's the way things are.

When I first got in the bond business, I undoubtedly cracked jokes that would have, a few years later, got me in trouble with the proper-speak and proper-thought proctors. Everyone, male and female, did. Usually it was fun, women gave as well as they got, and nobody was hurt. After I became a manager, I "evolved" to where I played it 100 percent straight, shedding the off-color jokes and insults.

I made good and bad women hires. Some I promoted, some I fired, and most I kept in the same position, just as I did with men. It was all business. Managing men and women working together is complicated and difficult, and I give myself a B grade. There were many things I could have done better.

The thing I never completely understood is how women interact with each other, especially in groups. Analyzing that is not for the squeamish. There is often subsurface tension, competition, and jealousy, all masked by an exquisite phoniness unique to the sex. I ventured that observation once to a female friend who had worked in—and left—an exclusively female job situation. Her response: "We are so closely aligned on this issue we might as well be one mind."

Keep the personal out of business and business out of the personal. Success in business doesn't automatically translate into success in courtship. I remember reading a letter to an advice columnist from a guy with an impressive resumé wondering why he could never get a second date. The columnist told him women don't fall for resumés, but qualities of personality and character, and gently suggested he address potential deficiencies there (like, perhaps, an inflated ego).

Men don't fall in love with resumés and business success either. No man has ever tumbled for a woman who gives good PowerPoint, although he may have admired any number of her attributes while she was giving her presentation. If he admired them enough he probably couldn't even remember, beyond getting a conversation started, what the PowerPoint was about.

I have heard women wonder why they or their friends, attractive and professionally accomplished, don't get asked out much. The standard explanation is that men are intimidated. Some men are, but often there are other reasons.

Men are turned off by women who can't stop talking about their jobs, bragging about their accomplishments, and most deadly, comparing themselves to, competing with, and implicitly or explicitly putting down the man in particular or men in general. Yes, woman have borne all that crap for centuries from men and payback is hell. However, if payback is a woman's mission and resentment her fuel, she shouldn't be surprised that men aren't lining up to woo her.

That may or may not matter to a woman. I don't pretend to know how women think, but I claim some expertise on my own sex. If a woman occasionally finds herself staring at a good-looking, well-built man and wondering what he'd be like in the sack, if she aches in a way that has only one remedy, if deep down she doesn't see what's so wrong with playful banter with the opposite sex and even, dare I say it, flirting, if she has found that interacting with men can be enjoyable, satisfying, even scintillating, if she's run into men who seem to have admirable qualities, and if she wonders if marriage and family really are just patriarchal traps; in short, if she's questioning the dogma that men are the enemy and all relations with them are inherently adversarial power struggles, perhaps I can offer a few words of advice.

All the indoctrination in the world isn't going to alter male biology. Eventually genetic engineering might, but until that sad day arrives, women should disabuse themselves of the fantasy that they're going to change the mass of men in any fundamental way. Youth and beauty will always spark their thunderbolts. Most women don't look like Simonetta Stefanelli (and most men don't look like Al Pacino). However, youth and beauty aren't the only arrows in the female quiver.

Men are drawn to just about every feature of the female anatomy. They'll leer at women's legs, boobs, butts, shoulders, backs, faces, eyes, hands, feet, and probably ears, noses, and throats. There is one anatomical feature with universal appeal: the smile. A smile will make the plainest face prettier, the woman more attractive. It can convey a million messages, often at the same time: joy, appreciation, flattery, confidence, irony, conspiracy, intimacy, invitation, mystery, and trust, to name a few. Man-hating feminists, acerbic academics, harpy politicians, and nannycrats don't smile at men, but confident women who welcome the opposite sex's challenges and opportunities do.

Smiling may sound like playing up to the male ego, and it is. I have yet to meet the male who doesn't have an ego, but I have yet to meet the female who doesn't have one either. Both sexes are susceptible to flattery from the opposite sex. Flash a smile and you may get one in return.

At its most elemental level, when a woman genuinely smiles at a man, she's saying I'm a woman and you are a man. At the end of the day—especially at the end of present days when women can be beating the pants off a man when he's out hunting mammoths—a man wants to come home to a woman who smiles, who is not a competitor, a preoccupied workaholic, a ball buster bent on his improvement, a political polemicist, or a cold fish.

He understood women and he understood now that Virginia was down because she thought he was having everything his own way. Women really hated seeing their men doing too well. It irritated them. It made them less sure of the hold they exerted over them through affection, sexual custom or marriage ties.

—The Godfather

Johnny Fontane's assessment of his ex-wife, Virginia, and women in general hit the nail on the head back in the 1940s.

Women's love was more pragmatic than men's, it had to be. Only a foolish woman would ignore a prospective mate's inability to provide and protect. Michael could allow his passion to overwhelm him, courting and marrying a younger woman of limited education who hardly spoke English; he wasn't going to be economically dependent on her. Women couldn't afford to chase thunderbolts, throwing judgment to the wind. If they were going to depend on a man they couldn't risk it all on a pretty face.

As women's love was more pragmatic, so too was their jealousy. Men required fidelity from their mates but not themselves, the infamous double standard. A man could reject an unfaithful wife; the woman didn't always have that option. It might mean supporting herself and her children with a low-paying job, or actual poverty. Even with alimony and child support it usually

101

meant a lower standard of living. So women like Virginia accepted their men's infidelities, hoping they were confined to casual, meaningless flings, and secretly feared their man's star shooting too high, propelled into an orbit filled with more beautiful, accomplished, and glamorous women—Margot Ashtons—who would threaten their status and lifestyles.

The old rules are gone (but not the old emotions), it's sexual anarchy. Men no longer have to forebear until marriage to have sex with "good" girls. Sex is readily available from good girls, bad girls, and girls in between with no commitment beyond the sex required or expected. Internet sites facilitate liaisons, or hook-ups as they're called, and for those men who would rather not bother with the intricacies and difficulties of the opposite sex, there's online pornography. For men looking for tactile gratification beyond their own hands and sex toys, sex dolls are ever-more lifelike. Anything goes.

Women can have sex without consequences via contraception, morning-after pills, or abortion. They don't have to rely on men for economic support, and if they decide to have children, they can raise them on their own or with the help or one or more people who are not the father. For many single mothers, the government chips in, with both cash and in-kind assistance—day care, meals, and schools.

People no longer have to hide a preference for their own sex. Indeed, anyone can chemically and surgically alter himself or herself so that they are herself or himself, and laws mandate that everyone else must accept the alteration. There are people who dress and act like men some days and women other days, depending on how they feel when they wake up. Anything goes.

Will the institution of marriage survive? Freedom from everything means commitment to nothing. Other than wanting to father children and bring them up in a stable, nurturing family, an increasingly quaint and deprecated notion, why would a man get married? It can be a huge economic burden and there's the ever-present risk of divorce and its financial and psychological devastation. Like illegitimacy, divorce no longer carries any stigma. The Internet is full of sites and commentators making the case for men against marriage. They are especially popular with young men.

To which an increasing number of women are saying good riddance. Who needs men except perhaps for sex, and women have access to the same online and mechanical substitutes as men. The brave new world of jobs and careers has opened up, which provides all the emotional fulfillment and economic empowerment a woman could ever want. It's a woman's choice to have children, and also her choice as to whether or not to keep the father around, even if that's his desire. Anything goes.

You would think that with all this freedom everyone would be happy, but the opposite is true. One of the best indicators of happiness is birthrates. People have children when times are good and they are happy and confident of the future. The birthrate drops during depressions, famines, wars, pestilence, and the other unhappy periods that occasionally beset humanity.

Across the Western world birthrates have dropped precipitously, to well below the replacement level of 2.1

children per couple, and are still dropping. There are undoubtedly a variety of reasons, but happiness and confidence in the future are not among them. And having fewer children means people have less of a stake in the future. Even ignoring the birthrate evidence, if our present day society is happy I'd hate to see unhappy.

Though people are not having as many children, the ones who make it bask in the glow of a sentimental veneration rivaled only by that showered on members of the military. We love our children! The entire village will raise them! You can get away with just about anything as long as you claim you're doing it for the children.

We love children so much that we don't have them if it might prove inconvenient. We love them so much we raise them with one parent. We love them so much we let friends, relatives, or complete strangers take care of them while we pursue careers and other interests. We love them so much we send them to government schools, where they're indoctrinated and receive lousy educations. We love them so much we saddle them with useless degrees and six-figure student loans. We love them so much we further saddle them with government debt and other promises that will never be kept to fund our wars—which they fight—our pensions, our medical care, and the interest on the debt we've incurred. We love them so much that we've crippled our economy and businesses with that debt, plus taxes, voluminous laws and regulations, and an ever-expanding government so that they can't get good jobs.

We sure do love our kids. And if they find themselves confused, resentful, angry and rebellious by this state of affairs, it's their fault. Many modern parents turn a neat trick, blaming either their parents or their kids, or both, for their own failings, but never themselves.

Why are so many people so unhappy? Because we're all part of the same hypocrisy, and the wages of hypocrisy are misery and chaos. It's not making it any easier for those of us who put in an honest day's work to conduct business and do our jobs. And it's ruining our lives and destroying our country.

Chapter 9

Il Capo dei Capi

That anyone would consider even for a moment killing a New York City police captain was too fantastic. The toughest hood in the Mafia had to stand still if the lowliest patrolman decided to slap him around. There was absolutely no percentage in killing cops.

—*The Godfather*

Mafia deference to cops stems from recognition that the government is *Il Capo dei Capi,* The Boss of Bosses, and cops are one of its front-line instruments. The government is the organized crime syndicate with the most muscle, uniquely endowed with the legal rights to steal, print money, and inflict violence. It wages wars and terrorizes its own citizens with impunity. Don Corleone recognizes the government's superior power and turns it to his own advantage. He's no different from legions of executives who lobby and bribe bureaucrats, legislators, and presidents for special laws, regulations, contracts, and subsidies to benefit their businesses and line their own pockets.

A government cannot tolerate attacks on its power any more than a Mafia don can. When Michael kills Captain McCluskey, the response is ferocious.

> *On the day after the murder of Sollozzo and Captain McCluskey, the police captains and lieutenants in every station house in New York City sent out the word: there would be no more gambling, no more prostitution, no more deals of any kind until the murderer of Captain McCluskey was caught. Massive raids began all over the city. All unlawful business activities came to a standstill.*

— *The Godfather*

For a brief time, future don Michael did more to stamp out New York crime than all the tough-on-crime politicians, prosecutors, and judges ever had. Of course "tough on crime" is always rhetoric. There's usually a direct relationship between the amount and fierceness of such rhetoric and how much the eminence who spews it is on the take. The criminals in the Mafia and New York's government were partners. Were the more equal partner to permanently shut down the less equal one, it would stop an important source of tribute. New York's war on rackets was short-lived—the police and *pezzonovantis* needed their bribes.

The government syndicate has its own rackets, and one of its most lucrative is criminalizing commerce.

Make trading in a good or service—drugs, firearms, sex—illegal and you've added a premium for those willing to run the risks of providing that good or service. That premium funds lifestyles the providers couldn't support pursuing legal endeavors, as well as the bribes that make the police and *pezzonovantis* their business partners.

There was almost no organized crime in this country before Prohibition. That legislation propelled the Godfather into the criminal underworld's elite.

> *When prohibition came to pass and alcohol forbidden to be sold, Vito Corleone made the final step from a quite ordinary, somewhat ruthless businessman to a great Don in the world of criminal enterprise. It did not happen in a day, it did not happen in a year, but by the end of the Prohibition period and start of the Great Depression, Vito Corleone had become the Godfather, the Don, Don Corleone.*

—The Godfather

Engaging in illegal enterprise removes those so engaged from the police and courts, the usual mechanisms for redressing crimes and settling business disputes. They have to provide their own remedies, which means violence. Success in criminal enterprise requires winning a race to the bottom—the ruthlessness to unflinchingly employ violence against innocents and fellow criminals alike. The Mafia left the drug business to Central and South American thugs because their violence was so excessive and cruel that even hardened mafiosi regarded it as barbaric.

No institution is more violent than government. During the last century governments around the globe whacked one hundred to two hundred million people, a tally that leaves everyone and everything else in the dust. Organized crime of all stripes partners with these apex criminals. Their mutually beneficial relationships are based on their shared propensity for violence. *Il Capo dei Capi* always gets the lion's share, but there's plenty left for the jackals.

An exact accounting is impossible, but by any reckoning the global trade in illegal drugs is in the hundreds of billions and perhaps trillions of dollars. It couldn't exist without the blessing and active support of governments: politicians, police, bureaucrats, and judges. This criminalized commerce flourishes with minimal government interference, no more than a nuisance and a necessary cost of business, easily borne by the drug growers, processors and distributors. It couldn't happen if every layer and division of government wasn't deeply compromised—on the take. If you scoff at that notion, well, *who's being naive, Kay?*

The US government monitors everything Americans do and no aspect of our lives is too trivial for it not to meddle, but somehow the drug trade thrives right under its nose. Recall the last time you heard of a prominent politician, government official, high-ranking police officer, or judge investigated for taking drug money or otherwise illegally aiding the drug trade, much less arrested, indicted, convicted or sentenced. You can't recall because it never happens. That's the dog that doesn't bark.

The arrests are confined to those caught up in headline-grabbing drug busts, the lowest levels of government, and the occasional cartel kingpin, thrown to the wolves as drug-government partnerships wage war against each other. The corruption is so deep, the illicit enrichment so vast, and the potential retribution so severe that anyone who dares investigate, challenge, or expose links between governments and the drug trade is almost certainly a goner.

Why do governments fight so hard against any kind of drug legalization? It would eliminate the risk premium that's the source of both drug industry profits and political payola. It has nothing to do with the risks, dangers and harms associated with drug use. Alcohol is risky, dangerous, and harmful—but legal—because it became obvious that Prohibition's funding of organized crime, the consequent political, judicial, and police corruption, and the widespread disrespect for and noncompliance with the law made Prohibition far more dangerous and harmful than that which it outlawed.

For decades there have been stories and scandals on the fringes that hint at the pervasiveness of the drug trade and its money laundering. Often such stories feature arms running and sexual trafficking in minors as well. The CIA and military in bed with drug operators in Vietnam during the 1960s and 1970s, and now in Afghanistan. The CIA fueling the crack cocaine epidemic in the US during the 1980s to fund the Nicaraguan Contras. A CIA-South American drug operation in the 1980s centered in this country at the

Mena, Arkansas airport, with alleged links to Presidents Reagan, H.W. Bush and Clinton, governor of Arkansas at the time. US government support for dictators and terrorist groups with known ties to drug operations. Bank scandals—the Bank of Credit and Commerce International, Nugan Hand Bank, Banco Ambrosiano, and the Hong Kong and Shanghai Bank Corporation, among others—that reveal drug money laundering and corrupt lending, global networks of political influence, and shadowy ties to various intelligence agencies, including the CIA and Mossad, the Israeli intelligence agency.

The stories sometimes find their way into the mainstream media but quickly fade. There are investigations, arrests, and even convictions. However, there are always tantalizing loose ends suggesting much deeper corruption and more extensive links to the "legitimate" world that are never pursued. Higher-level figures are rarely if ever prosecuted. And life goes profitably on for the drug and money laundering rackets, and the corrupt politicians, government officials, police, bankers, business people, and other cockroaches they support.

Incidentally, the War on Drugs illustrates a truism: if you want something to thrive, have the government declare war on it. President Nixon declared war on drugs and the drug trade is going gangbusters. President Johnson declared war on poverty and by most measures, poverty is at an all-time high. President George W. Bush declared war on terrorism, and there are far more America-hating terrorists out there now than when he made his declaration. If only the government would declare war on the American people, they might finally catch a break.

If a lawyer with his briefcase can steal more than a thousand gangsters with guns and masks, a Fortune 500 CEO with a team of good lawyers, lobbyists, and PACs can steal more than a thousand dons. Studies have shown that the highest return on investment for large corporations is not research and development, new products, new factories, advertising, or creating jobs. It's lobbying, by a large margin, which makes sense when you consider the differences between markets and the government.

In a free and open market, parties do business only if both parties benefit, there is no coercion involved. A business has to offer value for value, and there are always potential competitors should that business become too profitable. Someone may invent a better mousetrap that either reduces profit margins or puts it out of business altogether. It's no picnic competing every day for customer dollars.

Governments operate under no such constraints. When they want money, they steal, borrow, or print it. They can subsidize a company or pass laws and regulations that favor it and hamstring its competitors, buy goods and services at inflated prices, and fund wars, infrastructure projects, and other boondoggles that are enormously profitable for their business friends. Which is why so many people in businesses both legal and illegal seek to join forces with *Il Capo dei Capi*. Don Corleone could only dream of such powers.

What the government does *sub rosa* is disturbing, what it does every day out in the open far more so. Since the first OPEC oil embargo in 1973, you could compile volumes of officials' and politicians' statements about the dangers of that cartel and cartels in general, decrying the harm they do to economies, businesses, and ordinary people. Yet, promoting cartels is one thing the government does very well, it's a lucrative racket.

Look at the fools' paradise of regulation. A group of world-improvers decides that some problem with business can only be fixed by government regulation. They get laws and regulations passed. Then what happens? The world-improvers are on to the next crusade, and the affected businesses have to live with the regulation. What do they do?

They turn it to their own advantage! They hire lobbyists and lawyers to swarm the legislature and whatever alphabet agency has been set up to administer the law. There's nobody to oppose them. Businesses have money at stake; the world-improvers don't and they've moved on. Bribes, legal and otherwise, are offered and a revolving door installed between the agency and the businesses. Regulation can work all sorts of mischief: controlling prices, allocating markets, requiring expensive procedures and compliance that only well-established companies can afford, and making potential new entrants jump through a mind-numbing array of hoops and pay staggering costs before they can set up shop. In short, regulation promotes a cartel among the regulated.

"What I'm saying is that we have now what we've always needed, real partnership with the government."

—*Hyman Roth, Part Two*

Roth was extolling the Mafia's arrangements with the corrupt Cuban government to protect their hotels and casinos. Those were small change compared to the very real partnerships many "legitimate" businesses have now with the US government.

The biggest, most lucrative, and most brazen is the partnership of defense and high-tech outfits with the Department of Defense, the Department of Homeland Security, and the intelligence agencies. There are all sorts of off-budget and black box items so precision is impossible, but the government spends between $750 billion and $1 trillion annually on defense and intelligence. At the low end, that's almost three times as much as second-place China and over ten times as much as anyone else.

For that, we get a military that hasn't won a meaningful engagement since World War II and the Russians and Chinese reportedly have weapons that are superior to ours. We fight endless no-win wars in places like Afghanistan and only the contractors benefit. If that isn't a racket I don't know what is. Any doubts are dispelled with a tally of the many high-ranking military officers who retire from "serving the nation" and land as executives and directors with defense and intelligence companies, where the nation serves them munificent remuneration and cushy semi-retirements.

Defense is at the apex of a pyramid of cartels, the lower levels of which include state licensing requirements for things like hair-braiding and pumping gas and municipal garbage hauling and taxi franchises.

Many businesses big and small draw water from the government well.

At the federal level, the drug industry plays footsie with the Food and Drug Administration and the Centers for Disease Control and Prevention. The securities industry and the Securities and Exchange Commission (SEC) are a mutual admiration society. The large corporate farms and the Department of Agriculture send each other birthday and Christmas cards; the USDA puts big subsidy checks in theirs. If the banking industry and the Federal Reserve were any more affectionate they'd have to get a room.

I had a bird's eye view of that cartel in action during the financial crisis of 2008-2009. Our financial system promotes the never-ending expansion of debt, which guarantees it will occasionally fail. Banks, securities firms, and other financial operators speculate on all manner of instruments with borrowed money far in excess of their equity capital. Before the financial crisis some of them had borrowed more than thirty times their capital to finance speculation, notably on housing, mortgages, and mortgage-backed securities. Everything was hunky dory as long as house prices were rising, but as we keep rediscovering, nothing goes up forever.

Once prices started to fall, it wasn't long before highly leveraged (borrowing a lot of money compared to capital) financial institutions began failing. If you borrow $24 for every dollar of your own capital that you put up on a speculation (96 percent leverage) it only takes a 4 percent move against you to wipe out your capital. At the height of the crisis, some markets were dropping more than 4 percent in a single day.

All sorts of pass-the-buck artists and talking heads said nobody could have seen the financial crisis coming. That's pure hog slop. With 96 percent leverage it's a question of when and not if a trade blows up.

The global economy is based on debt. Every debt, or borrower's liability, is a creditor's asset. When trades financed by borrowed money start blowing up, so too do creditors, and it can reach an inflection point where it quickly spreads throughout our financially interconnected world. There were plenty of articles before the blow-up warning that it was coming. Plain old common sense was also helpful during this time, like asking: *what if house prices fall?* Some answered correctly, put their money where their answers were, and made fortunes.

The world has more debt now than it did then, so another blow-up is assured. Because there's more debt, the next one will be worse than the last one. You heard it here first: when it arrives, all sorts of people will claim nobody could have seen it coming.

During the last crisis, I was rooting for the banks to fail and the financial system to collapse, and not just because I had placed my bets on that outcome. The US monetary system is built on the fraud of an unbacked currency that the Federal Reserve produces at will. The government issues unlimited amounts of debt which the Federal Reserve buys with its currency, technically a debt of the Federal Reserve (Federal Reserve *Notes*—a note is a debt instrument).

The US economy is based on the government's and central bank's ever-expanding debt. Serving as profitable middlemen to these shell games are the big

116

banks. An important mission of their sugar daddy, the Federal Reserve, is to not let them fail when the debt-based charade falls apart, as it must from time to time.

Failure is the essential flip side of success in capitalism. Most of us aren't issued guarantees against failure, and most of us have failed at least once. We dust ourselves off and start over. Stuck as it is in the quicksand of a fraudulent currency, ever-expanding debt, and heads-we-win-tails-the-American-taxpayer-gets-screwed crony socialism, the financial system needs to collapse completely so we can replace it with something better. It's the host for a myriad of financial parasites and needs to die, taking the parasites with it. That's what I was rooting for. Call it a longing for justice.

Of course that didn't happen. There were bailouts and TARP, financed with more debt. The Federal Reserve and every other central bank in the world flooded the system with even more debt at very low or negative interest rates, pulling favored institutions out of the holes they had dug for themselves. All that debt has fueled massive assets bubbles: Exhibits A and B are the US stock and bond markets.

The crony socialists don't even have the decency to lay low and not draw attention to their heists. They show up on TV or giving interviews to financial scribes, praising themselves and their corrupt system for "saving" the US and the world from the "unforeseen" financial Armageddon they were so instrumental in almost bringing about.

And I'm still rooting.

In my naiveté, I thought the financial crisis would be a boon to my firm. We had been the financial paragon that had eschewed debt, turned down offers to hop on the mortgage and mortgage securities' gravy train, issued repeated warnings on the impending crisis, placed our bets on it, and made money when so many had staggering losses that should and would have wiped them out, but for the government. Surely new customers and brokers would flock to us. We were the firm that could stand on its own, that didn't need a bailout. I invested more money in the partnership.

That didn't work out too well. Customers and brokers were drawn to companies that had received the prized Too Big To Fail label during the crisis. Why go with a small firm based on sound financial values when you could sign up with a behemoth guaranteed by the government? The TBTF's had a field day, and we found the going harder than before the crisis.

To add insult to injury, the SEC decided our little company—whose annual revenue amounted to less than a big bank's daily cash flow—posed a clear and present danger to the global financial system, and we were struck with a plague of regulatory locusts. I can't prove it, but I suspect the TBTFs were using the SEC to consolidate control of the industry, targeting the small fry.

The SEC hounded us to outsource our operations department to one of the larger firms. Admittedly, our back office was an antiquated mess, but it was just inefficient, not dangerous.

Although my department had made money on credit default swaps during the crisis, I was called into several meetings with SEC regulators to first explain and then justify our speculation in those instruments (making money was an insufficient justification). Credit default swaps are arcane, so it took a long time to get past step one. Eventually they left me alone, but our managing partner, controller, and director of operations were not so blessed, wasting valuable hours in pointless meetings. Meanwhile, the TBTFs paid some fines, revised a few procedures and practices, and skated free.

And I'm still rooting.

"Senator, we're both part of the same hypocrisy."

—Part Two

We're all part of Senator Geary and Michael Corleone's hypocrisy. Its wellspring is the age-old desire: something for nothing. The government can supposedly give us stuff and nobody has to pay for it. While few people would walk up to John Q. Taxpayer and steal his money at gunpoint, most people have no problem when the government does if for them. That's the hypocrisy.

Anything the government gives to us is taken from someone else. Government is force, which produces nothing, it only plunders. The Washington D.C. metropolitan area is the nation's richest. Most of what the government steals it keeps for itself and its accomplices, while reserving enough to bribe a sufficient percentage of voters to stay in control.

A political monopoly protects the government syndicate's cartels and rackets. Politicians use the powers of government to cement their own power; incumbents rarely lose elections. Most politicians leave office far wealthier than when they were first elected. When they retire from "public service," they often become highly paid lobbyists, wheedling favors and loot from their fellow criminals still in government.

For over a hundred years now, it hasn't mattered which party was in power. The government has gotten bigger, more powerful, and more intrusive regardless. It makes perpetual war to the profit of its cronies, who recycle part of those profits back to officials and politicians. Stealing money from the productive, it buys the votes of the unproductive. What it allows itself to do expands without limit while what it allows the people to do keeps shrinking. It already knows most everything we do, say, and think. Taxes, laws, regulations, and debt pile up on the overburdened population.

> *He had a fleet of freight hauling trucks that made him a fortune primarily because his trucks could travel with a heavy overload and not be stopped and fined by highway weight inspectors. These trucks helped ruin the highways and then his road-building firm, with lucrative state contracts, repaired the damage wrought. It was the kind of operation that would warm any man's heart, business of itself creating more business.*

—*The Godfather*

The *Capo dei Capi* takes it one step farther than Mafia don Anthony Stracci. Like Stracci's, the government's corrupt business creates more corrupt business for itself. However, if Stracci's racket ever became common knowledge, Stracci might have to put up with some unpleasantness. Many of the government's rackets are out in the open for all to see, and yet fools and knaves demand still more. Even most of the intelligent and honest stay quiet. The fools and knaves call on government to solve problems that government created. Some demand socialism, putting it in complete control.

Where there are votes and a political demand, politicians will fill it, and those who love government have a growing number of votes. Many of them were educated in government schools, which have instilled in them a belief in government—a corrupt business creating more corrupt business for itself.

Start a business, from a dog walking service on up, and you'll soon run into the government. I'm involved with a startup whose technology is just now making it from the laboratory to prototypes and an agency of the federal government and a state government have already expressed interest.

As a municipal bond trader, I was dealing with bonds—debt—issued by governments. I was one of many traders who made what is called a secondary market in those bonds. The availability of a secondary market facilitates the government's issuance of bonds, which is called the primary market. Nobody would buy debt from an issuer if there weren't a secondary market for them to trade that debt afterwards. I helped make it easier for municipalities to issue debt.

That was the only involvement with municipal governments I wanted. Over the course of my career, all sorts of people thought my training as a lawyer and my experience as a municipal bond trader would make me the ideal public finance banker. A public finance banker solicits municipalities for their bond business and negotiates the deals. I always declined.

I don't like politicians and bureaucrats, and the public finance business is corrupt. The local poobahs who award municipal bond deals are generally hacks with an outsize appreciation of themselves. Winning deals means not just attending their many meetings, but wining, dining, and enduring, far into the night, the fascinating stories of their fascinating lives. It means payola, both above board and under the table. When I was at the Wall Street firm, I had to write personal checks to politicians I had never heard of so the firm's bankers would have a shot at lucrative municipal bond deals.

All the corrupt lucrativeness of the public finance business could be sucked right out of it if municipalities simply conducted open, competitive bidding among underwriting syndicates for their bond issues. Study after study has shown that competitive bidding produces lower interest costs than negotiated deals for municipal issuers. When I first got in the business, new issues were split about 50-50 between competitive and negotiated deals. Not surprisingly, issuance has shifted towards the latter. Nowadays most issues are negotiated.

The poobahs love the wining, dining, and payola. Firms like the higher interest rates and larger underwriting spreads they negotiate with the issuers they've bribed—you've got to be an incompetent moron to lose money on a negotiated deal. Underwriting a competitive deal was never a sure thing and I lost money on plenty of them.

When I went to the private partnership to run its bond department, I received suggestions that I set up a public finance unit. I said I wouldn't do it because the business was corrupt. To the partnership's credit, that was all the explanation required to keep it out of public finance.

The government is so pervasive that everyone in business has to make decisions about how much involvement they will have with it. Some involvement, like regulations and taxes, is involuntary. However, if the government wants to buy what you're selling, you have to decide if and how you want to dance with the devil.

The *Capo dei Capi* plays by its own rules, which can change in a heartbeat. While there is a rough code of honor within *The Godfather*, the government has none. Its word is not its bond. Appearances are invariably deceiving. Today's friend can become tomorrow's enemy for reasons you cannot fathom. There's always someone more ruthless and corrupt than you plotting to steal your business.

James Hill was an actual Industrial Revolution railroad titan who makes an appearance in my novel, *The Golden Pinnacle*. I put fictional words in his mouth that should be prominently posted on the office walls of every business person in the world.

"If you crawl into bed with the government, you're laboring under a delusion as to who's doing the poking and who's getting poked."

— *The Golden Pinnacle*

123

Chapter 10

Sicily

Vito Corleone stashes Peter Clemenza's guns, hiding them from the police. Out of gratitude, Clemenza gives him a rug after enlisting him to help steal it. In *Part Two*, lighthearted music opens the scene as the two break into a fine apartment. They elude discovery by a curious policeman at the front door, roll up the carpet, and to the strains of more lighthearted music carry it through the streets to Vito's tenement apartment. The Godfather's life of crime has begun.

Actually there's nothing lighthearted about their theft of the rug. If your home has ever been burgled, you know the rage and sense of violation the owners would feel when they discover it's been stolen.

Vito joins Clemenza and Tessio in a gang that hijacks trucks transporting dresses from the factory where they are stitched together. Times are hard and work is scarce. His first theft is low risk and he clears $700, a lot of money in 1919. However, Fanucci, the neighborhood extortionist, demands a share of the loot.

In later years Vito Corleone understood that what had made him act in such a perfect, tactical way with Fanucci was the death of his own hot-tempered father who had been killed by the Mafia in Sicily. But at that time all he felt was an icy rage that this man planned to rob him of the money he had risked his life and freedom to earn.

—The Godfather

Fanucci had no right to Vito's money, but neither did Vito. He had risked his life and freedom to *steal*, not *earn* it, and Fanucci tried to extort it from him. They're both thieves. The dressmaker is denied the honest profit he would have *earned*, and the prices of the dresses he does sell will be higher to cover the costs of stolen merchandise, increased security, and insurance. That takes money from his honest customers, and fences will sell his dresses to less scrupulous buyers at cut-rate prices, from which the dressmaker will get nothing.

There are elements of an inspiring rags-to-riches story in Mario Puzo's account of the Godfather's rise. However, the Godfather's criminality doesn't fit in such a story. He goes into the olive oil business, but rather than compete on the merits, he burns his competitors' warehouses and dumps their trucks carrying olive oil. An aggrieved competitor who goes to the authorities— the approved course of action for aggrieved business people—is murdered.

Puzo had a problem. In real life Mafia hoods are unappealing people who do unappealing things, more like Luca Brasi than either of the Don Corleones. He took dramatic license to make his Mafiosi more palatable. To move his characters closer to legitimate businessmen, he uses the language of commerce. Characters talk about their business, their work, and making a living, not their rackets, thefts, extortions, frauds, swindles, or other crimes. Never mentioned is that they're depriving innocents of their money and property—their living—by stealing from them.

> *"Well, when the boss says push a button on a guy, I push a button. See Senator?"*

> *—Willi Cicci to Senate Committee Chairman, Part Two*

Cicci's "push a button" is clinical, it sounds much better than "I blow people's brains out from close range" or even "I murder people" would. Besides making Puzo's dons, *caporegimes*, and button-men more palatable, such sleight of hand reflects an insight: in their own minds evil people enhance their self-images with euphemistic diversion. Shut out the correct words and maybe you shut out ugly reality and loathsome self-awareness. A euphemism is a flashing sign: *check under the hood before you drive this one off the lot*.

No surprise, then, that government, the most vile and evil institution on the planet, is also the most blatant and prolific purveyor of euphemisms and other linguistic sleight-of-hand. Since World War II, the US has waged more offensive wars than any other country, hasn't fought a single defensive battle against a foreign invader, and yet we have a *Department of Defense*.

Missiles are *Peacekeepers,* changing an autocratic regime for one more to our liking *promotes democracy,* torture is *enhanced interrogation,* moving someone to another country to be tortured is *rendition,* destroying a village *saves* it, wiping out neighborhoods for the benefit of crony developers is *redevelopment,* taxes are *user fees,* higher taxes are *revenue enhancement,* boondoggles are *investments,* unearned money from the government is an *entitlement,* making health care more expensive makes it *affordable,* quotas promote *equal opportunity,* and so on and so on and so on.

Fittingly, one of the most ignominious linguistic evasions is carved above the entrance to the Internal Revenue Service building in Washington: *Taxes are what we pay for a free society.* That quote is attributed to Justice Oliver Wendell Holmes Jr. Pushed to its logical extreme, when the government takes everything you make, you'll be 100 percent free.

Somehow the government managed during its first 137 years, except during the Civil War and immediately afterwards, to get by without income taxes and the country didn't descend into barbarism. Quite the opposite, as the US during that period went from a nation of small farmers, artisans, and merchants to become the world's preeminent economic power and the destination of choice for millions of non-freeloading immigrants.

Crime is a lot easier when the victims don't realize they're victims. The government and the Mafia are parasites, living off the work of those who honestly produce. Linguistic contortions are designed to obscure that fact from parasites and victims alike. Like other parasites, organized crime and governments weaken and often kill the hosts.

We have left not quite to the last the richest of all the regions colonized by the Greeks. To Sicily nature had given what she had withheld from continental Greece — an apparently inexhaustible soil fertilized by rain and lava, and producing so much wheat and corn that Sicily was thought to be if not the birthplace at least a favorite haunt of Demeter herself. Here were orchards, vineyards, olive groves, heavy with fruit; honey as succulent as Hymettus', and flowers blooming in their turn from the beginning to the end of the year. Grassy plains pastured sheep and cattle, endless timber grew in the hills, and the fish in the surrounding waters reproduced faster than Sicily could eat them.

—*The Life of Greece,* Will Durant, 1939, Simon and Schuster

Many centuries ago, Sicily was a paradise. Unfortunately, the island's natural bounty and central Mediterranean location made it an irresistible target for successive invaders. Sicilians perpetually suffered under governments whose first concern was never the well-being of the governed.

Sicily was a land that had been more cruelly raped than any other in history. The Inquisition had tortured rich and poor alike. The landowning barons and the princes of the Catholic Church exercised absolute power over the shepherds and farmers. The police were the instruments

*of their power and so identified with them that to be
called a policeman is the foulest insult one Sicilian can
hurl at another.*

—*The Godfather*

Ordinary Sicilians banded together against their
oppressors. The word "Mafia" originally meant a place
of refuge. It became the name for the secret organization
that fought the tyrannical rulers. Observing *omerta*, the
law of silence, Sicilians stoically bore their subjugation.

*A woman whose husband had been murdered would not
tell the police the name of her husband's murderer, not
even of her child's murderer, her daughter's raper.*

—*The Godfather*

Like Amerigo Bonasera, they went to their Mafia dons
for justice. Some delivered, some didn't. Unfortunately,
from its Robin Hood-like roots the Mafia became a tool
for the corrupt government and aristocracy. It was more
profitable and less dangerous to align with the rulers
than fight them, and the Mafia became another
instrument of oppression. With both the government
and the Mafia preying on the people, one of the world's
most beautiful and bountiful lands deteriorated into one
of its most lawless and violent.

Michael walks through Corleone, his father's home
village that gave him his last name. All the men are dead
from vendettas. The Sicily to which Michael flees is a

desiccated shell, juices sucked dry by the parasite rulers and Mafia.

> *Sicily was already a land of ghosts, its men emigrating to every other country on earth to be able to earn their bread, or simply to escape being murdered for exercising their political and economic freedoms.*

> — *The Godfather*

Any honest, productive man faced with the near certainly that whatever he produced would be stolen, and the absolute certainty that if he complained he'd be dead, could either join the degenerative battle of all against all—risking death by vendetta—or emigrate. Nothing was left in Sicily for those who wanted to build something for themselves. This is what violence had wrought—life's promise was gone.

Look at a map of the United States that shows topography and natural resources. Bounded by the Atlantic and Pacific to the east and west, sparsely inhabited Canada to the north, and Mexico to the south, the U.S. has built-in protection against the invasions that have wracked countries in Asia and Europe for centuries. American ships reap bounties from the oceans and trade. They dock at deep water ports on both the east and west coasts, and sail on one of the world's most extensive networks of navigable rivers.

The country has oil, ores, timber, water, arable land, and minerals in abundance, raw materials for its awesomely productive agriculture and industry. There are towering mountain ranges, vertiginous canyons, spectacular sea shores, verdant forests, gigantic lakes, and plains and deserts that stretch to the horizon in all directions.

It seems inevitable that ambitious, energetic, capable people, freed from the shackles that had bound them in the lands from whence they came, would build a great and prosperous nation, and they did. It seems impossible that it could be ruined, but it has been. How long before the United States is another Sicily?

The US government and its partners in crime grow ever more corrupt and violent. Most people don't want to acknowledge it, much less contemplate where it's leading. Corruption and violence always wreak decay, destruction, and death. You can get a preview of coming attractions in, among other places, our nightmarish inner cities, squalid homeless encampments, and rural towns and villages abandoned to the opioid addicted and those who sell to them.

There were probably Sicilian shepherds who in their own way fought the forces of darkness. Americans mostly resemble their sheep. The government steals more of their money, freedom, privacy, and heritage every year and only isolated voices are raised in protest. The *pezzonovantis* grow increasingly grasping, secretive, and repressive.

It used to be taken for granted that the dynamic and innovative US economy would expand and American workers could look forward to rising wages and better lives for themselves and their children. Wages after inflation have stagnated for more than two decades and the long-term economic growth trend has been down.

The reported growth numbers are overstated, because most such "growth" is bought with the national credit card. The growth numbers treat what's bought on that card as national income, but it's income in the same way that your new credit card charges are.

Average pay in the government is higher than it is in the private sector, and the pensions and medical benefits are better, too. The government taxes and borrows over $4 trillion a year. Washington is the nation's richest metropolitan area. *Il Capo dei Capi*, its many rackets, and the *pezzonovantis* are indeed thriving. However, in the history of parasitism, no parasite has ever realized that it would be in its long-term best interest to keep the host alive. Washington's are no different and they're killing the host.

At over $22 trillion, the government's debt is now greater than the gross domestic product, and the government's debt plus unfunded liabilities—promises of future benefits for things like Social Security and Medicare—are, by conservative estimates, over $124 trillion (see usdebtclock.org). What that means is that every American is on the hook for over $375,000. If debt and unfunded liabilities are allocated just to taxpayers, they are on the hook for over one million dollars apiece. This at a time when the Baby Boom generation is retiring, drawing on Social Security, Medicare, and other programs for the elderly, and the ratio of younger workers to retirees is shrinking. Bankruptcy looms.

Michael thought about his father's organization. If it continued to prosper it would grow into what had

132

happened here on this island, so cancerous that it would destroy the whole country.

—The Godfather

With the spending and debt, plus the taxes we must pay and the hundreds of thousands of laws and regulations we must obey, is it any wonder that our economy suffers from a wasting disease, or that our politics has become a battle of all against all? This is what happens when organized crime—the government and its subsidiary and allied rackets—takes over. It is cancerous, killing the country.

Like any criminal organization, the government has its secrets, and woe to anyone who reveals them. Ask Julian Assange, Edward Snowden, or Chelsea Manning. Every year the government classifies tens of thousands of documents. Many of those documents are classified not because they'd compromise national security in any way, but because they'd embarrass or incriminate somebody. Even obtaining documents that aren't classified entails wasting time and money jumping through the hoops. The law says the government has to disclose them, but the reality is often interminable foot-dragging.

Undoubtedly the secrecy cloaks illicit and criminal acts. We see only a small part of what actually goes on with our government. Much the news media has become its mouthpiece. Not only does it not ask questions or investigate wrongdoing, it has become a cog in the government's proper-speak and proper-thought propaganda machinery. You get in trouble for revealing secrets, but you also get in trouble for asking questions or stating truths obvious to anyone who cares to look...and think. Opening people's eyes is now a subversive act.

Totalitarian governments try to control everything people say, do, and think. High technology and social media companies have become *Il Capo dei Capi*'s surveillance and enforcement arm. America's *pezzonovantis* have far more power over ordinary people than Sicily's did at the island's corrupt worst. They monitor your communications, purchases, movements, friends, beliefs, and political affiliations. They've got reams of information with which they can blackmail you, and reams of laws and regulations they can charge you with violating.

If you think that you've got nothing to worry about because you've done nothing wrong, well, *who's being naive, Kay?* People who have done nothing wrong lose their lives, money, property, and even their children to the government all the time. Google *no-knock raids, civil asset forfeiture,* and *child endangerment.*

> *Michael Corleone understood for the first time why men like his father chose to become thieves and murderers rather than members of the legal society. The poverty and fear and degradation were too awful to be acceptable to any man of spirit.*

—*The Godfather*

The *pezzonovantis* increase their power, line their pockets, control information, and threaten ordinary people. Thanks to the Internet and outlets that have not yet been completely blocked, a growing number of people realize they are parasitic criminals and the government is organized crime.

Soon the poverty and fear and degradation will be too awful to be acceptable to any man or woman of spirit. We won't have the Sicilian solution of emigration. Most of the world is no better off, and the few semi-free refuges out there could only take a tiny percentage of our population. We don't have to become thieves or murderers, but resistance will be outlawed and resisters will be criminals.

The choice confronts each one of us: fight or fold?

Chapter 11

This Book Will Not Make You Rich

At UCLA and UC Berkeley, I ran into students and professors who had nothing good to say about wealth or the wealthy. Even back in the 1970s and 1980s there were plenty of campus socialists. The schemes of these self-proclaimed geniuses involved stealing from the despised but productive wealthy, who would nevertheless continue to produce, supposedly for the greater good rather than their own profit.

I emerged from those cockamamie campus cocoons to a world where ideas had to make sense, nothing was produced without work, and the bright, ambitious, and industrious competed for life's limited rewards. I met people who had made fortunes. Some I despised for their personalities or the way they had acquired their wealth, or both. Some I admired, the ones whose wealth had come honestly and hadn't warped their personalities. Invariably they embodied extraordinary qualities of character. Regardless of what MBA program literature, business tomes, and get-rich-quick videos say, you don't pick up those qualities from a school, book, or video.

Anybody who thinks making an honest fortune is easy (I had a professor at UCLA who insisted it was) has never tried it. I'm involved with a startup as an investor and executive. We're bringing to market technologies invented by a genius: a Cal Tech Ph.D., rocket scientist, and retired Princeton professor. His inventions have applications in at least ten different billion-dollar industries, so the potential is there. However, taking ideas from a laboratory to commercially viable products is filled with false starts and frustration infrequently interrupted by the achievement of significant milestones.

Even when the ideas are extraordinary. Our inventor's patented spray nozzle puts a charge on a fluid; the fluid's droplets are charged when they leave the nozzle. It sounds simple and conceptually it is. I understand the technology and I'm not an engineer or scientist. However, the engineering and physics principles behind it are complex and charging droplets opens up a world of possibilities.

Because droplets are like-charged, they repel and speed away from each other. They also go to ground, the target being sprayed. The spray wraps around the target, covering front, back, top, bottom, and irregular surfaces without moving either the sprayer or the target. The coat is uniform and there is little aerosol drift or overspray. There are substantial cost savings with fewer environmental and health and safety hazards.

Stick the nozzle on the end of a fuel injector and fuel will disperse better within the combustion chamber than current fuel injection allows. It will burn more completely and could achieve at least a 5 percent efficiency gain, millions of gallons of fuel saved every day. There would be a corresponding reduction in noxious exhaust gas and particulate waste emissions. We're currently working with another company to develop that application.

You can check out the company and technology at www.4rysprays.com. Brilliant as that technology may be, there are a lot of bright people and good ideas out there competing for investor and customer dollars. Most people have no idea of the brains embedded in the products and services that make it to the marketplace, that are profitable, that *succeed*. There are bright ideas embedded in many that fail.

Think about a simple doorknob and lock mechanism. Do you know how it works? Could you replace it, much less make it on your own? The world is filled with inventions that make life more livable and which we take for granted. Most of us have no idea how they work or what goes into producing them.

Business is an intricate and dynamic interplay of knowledge, ideas, innovation, people, products, competition, companies, and industries. The people who succeed, even in well-established industries, usually do so because they do something differently, and better, than their competitors. They see products, services, markets, or ways to organize their companies that no one else sees.

Vito Corleone was a man with vision. All the great cities of America were being torn by underworld strife.

138

Guerrilla wars by the dozen flared up, ambitious hoodlums trying to carve themselves a bit of empire; men like Corleone himself were trying to keep their borders and rackets secure. Don Corleone saw that the newspapers and government agencies were using these killings to get stricter and stricter laws, to use harsher police methods. He foresaw that public indignation might even lead to a suspension of democratic procedures which could be fatal to him and his people. His own empire, internally, was secure. He decided to bring peace to all the warring factions in New York City and then in the nation.

—The Godfather

It requires not-to-be-learned-from-books-or-schools smarts and imagination even to rise to the top of organized crime.

Like other great rulers and lawgivers in history Don Corleone decided that order and peace were impossible until the number of reigning states had been reduced to a manageable number.

—The Godfather

Using diplomacy and instruments of terror Sonny Corleone and Luca Brasi, the Don subdued or eliminated warring factions and imposed a reign of relative peace and harmony on New York City. This laid the groundwork for a "working agreement among the most powerful organizations in the country." That agreement held up through World War II and was only breached when Virgil Sollozzo tried to murder the Don. While it was in force, the Corleone family and the other Mafia families prospered.

Imagination is always in short supply in business. Having a vision and then making it a reality requires both brains and balls. The Godfather "had no illusions about the dangerousness of his mission." He took substantial risks pursuing his peace initiative among what were, after all, a bunch of thugs. Any number of things could have gone wrong, including his assassination. Only after the risks were run could he enjoy the fruits of his peace.

Most people don't even have the courage to reach their full intellectual potential—the balls to be brainy. It starts in childhood, where the bright kids are labelled nerds and the occasional outbreaks of intelligence are mocked. Harassing and beating up nerds is an endless source of amusement, especially for the cool kids. I grew up in Los Alamos, home of the atomic bomb and perhaps the planet's highest per capita concentration of Ph.D.s. You'd think it would be a haven for nerds, but even there, nerd kids got little respect. I was bright but not off the charts. I did my best to hide my brains and any nerdish tendencies.

Some nerds slough off the abuse, grow up, go to top-notch colleges and grad schools, enter difficult and intellectually challenging fields, lead satisfying lives, and achieve their full potential. Sadly, some don't. However, no matter where you go or what you do, social pressure to conform your thinking to the herd's, and especially not to make the herd look stupid, never goes away.

As with most startups, the one with which I'm involved is constantly trying to raise money. We deal with the venture capital crowd. Success in that field requires finding unique businesses that will eventually be profitable. Yet, a lot of venture capital seems as fashion-driven as, well, the fashion industry. As in any industry, I'm sure successful venture capital firms do things differently than their peers. However, many of the venture capitalists, or VCs, I've met speak fluent buzzword and are obsessed with trendy concepts. Not surprisingly, the profession is loaded with MBAs.

There is a standard progression. An interested VC will first ask for your pitch deck, a slide presentation with ten to fifteen slides that sums up your business. If that doesn't quell the VC's interest, you'll submit your business plan. From that, the three things of most interest to the VC will be your financial projections, the proposed terms of investment, and your exit strategy.

The financial projections, from three to five years out, are exercises in fantasy. It's usually required that you show rapid growth and profits within a year or two, the exceptions being certain well-backed Silicon Valley darlings that seemingly never have to book a profit. Fantasy though they may be, many VCs treat financial projections as if they were Moses' tablets.

The terms of investment are the only part of the business plan that admits of any precision. Business owners will set out exactly what they need and how much of the company they're willing to give up to get it.

The VCs will want to know the company's exit strategy, which is another exercise in fantasy. The owners will say they plan to sell the company or take it public in a few years at a drawn-from-a-hat valuation that is a mouth-watering multiple of the valuation the investors will pay for their share of the company. The VCs take great comfort from exit strategies; they're the pot of gold at the end of the rainbow. It's always rainbows when you talk with VCs, you don't mention dark clouds or thunderstorms. If they like your rainbows, they'll come up with a counterproposal to your terms and an agreement may eventually be negotiated and signed.

My experience is limited, but I can offer three pieces of advice in dealing with VCs. Avoid Silicon Valley; run, don't walk, from the bovine stare, and try to deal with people who are at least fifty-years old.

Silicon Valley is a wonder of the world. The problem is that its inhabitants know it, and bask in their transcendent specialness. They're smarter, better informed, better connected, and more sophisticated than you. You do realize, don't you, that there are thousands of people and companies who want their time and money? You'd better be damn grateful for the thirty seconds they give you for your elevator pitch.

I've had Silicon Valley types complete my sentences (always with different words than the ones I had in mind) or walk away from me in mid-sentence. Lest you think that might be because I'm a leaden or dimwitted speaker, I know bright, articulate people who've experienced the same thing. When Silicon Valley VCs request materials from you and decide they're not interested, they don't let you know that. Being Silicon Valley, many of their submissions processes are automated over the Internet, but somehow they can't automate a reply: *Thanks, but no thanks.*

The bovine stare comes from potential investors who ask a question or two and decide your company doesn't float their boat. You're babbling on and they're thinking about where they're going for lunch. They don't ask any further questions, stare bovinely at some fixed point behind you, and at the first appropriate pause exit the conversation. Out of politeness they may ask you to send them your materials, but that's a guaranteed waste of time.

What you want is somebody with real-life experience outside the MBA-VC universe who asks a ton of questions and demonstrates a keen interest and intellect. Such people are generally older. VC's advertise themselves as not just sources of money, but of contacts and business expertise. There's not a startup in the world who can't use all three, but that pitch means a lot more coming from someone who's put kids through college than it does from someone who's fresh out of grad school. Ultimately, if you have an idea or invention that can make it in the market, you'll have to find VCs who have the same combination of brains, imagination, and balls that it takes to succeed in other endeavors.

Great VCs and great traders capitalize on what I call the big trades. By definition, almost nobody recognizes a big trade until well after it has begun. The VC sees immense profit potential in a startup everyone else has ignored. The trader sees that a long-running trend which everyone believes will continue is actually primed for an explosive reversal.

> *"The crowd never thinks. People are only comfortable in a pack, and they're most comfortable in one that's racing off a cliff."*

—*The Golden Pinnacle*

Herd-think is an essential element of big trades. Speculation and investment are exercises in crowd psychology. It takes brains to recognize a big trade before it happens, but it also takes the balls to ignore the herd, which is why few people ever make even one big trade. Breaking from the herd, you place your bet, perhaps lose some money for a while—at least on paper—and patiently wait for the herd to come to you.

One attractive feature of a big trade is that the returns are so outsize they don't require a huge investment or leverage to generate jaw-dropping profits. You need not go all in on a big trade. Multiplying your original stake as they do, big trades require only a small, comfortably safe portion of your investment capital. You are doing the opposite of what everyone else has already done, which means the prevailing trend doesn't have much more to run. Consequently, your downside is limited.

Once you've made your bet, the hardest part is staying with it when things start going your way. The annals of speculation and investment are filled with stories of people who covered their winning bets way too soon. The price doubles or triples, they sell, and the price keeps going, to levels that represent large multiples of their realized profit. One of the initial investors in John D. Rockefeller's Standard Oil was offered cash or stock for his stake and took cash. He built a mansion, but with what those shares in Standard would have eventually been worth he could have built a town full of mansions. Early on, an Apple founder sold his stake for a pittance of its later value.

Profits mess with your head. You alternate between exultation as the market moves your way and your profits pile up, and anxiety that you'll lose those fabulous profits when the market occasionally jiggles the other way. One of my big trades was buying put options on a stock index future—a bet the stock market would go down—in 2008 just before Lehman Brothers failed. I made a substantial profit on them, but the volatility tore my stomach to shreds and I didn't sleep much for a couple of weeks. I bought the puts at $2.75 and sold the last of them after they had first reached $100, to my delight, dropped to $80, to my despair, and recovered to $100—in less than an hour! Shaken by the volatility, I sold them there, but had I waited two days I could have sold them for over $200.

Big trades aren't always financial. Almost everybody has shoulda, coulda, wouldas: the career they didn't pursue, the job offer they didn't accept, the person they didn't date or marry. Through some lack of foresight or fortitude, we miss opportunities that would have had big psychic, emotional, and perhaps monetary payoffs. What's especially wrenching is when we suspected at the time we were making a mistake.

Michael Corleone scores a big trade when he has the heads of New York's five families and assorted other

Corleone family enemies murdered as he stands godfather to Carlo Rizzi and his sister Connie's son. It's rightly considered one of the greatest scenes in cinema. Later that day, Michael murders Carlo and Tessio. In one masterstroke Michael goes from the not particularly feared head of the Corleone family in decline to the most powerful Mafia boss in New York and the nation.

Then there are the trades with the opposite risk and reward profile of a big trade. Anti-big trades entail huge risks, often taken out of desperation and conscience, for little potential gain or actual loss. Whether it's challenging the school bully, hiding Jews in the attic, or refusing to sit in the back of the bus, stands on principle are the heart of many great stories. Unfortunately, most of them don't have a Hollywood ending, which accounts for their scarcity in real life.

> *"Does this man have real balls?"*
> *Hagen considered exactly what the Don meant by this question. Over the years he had learned that the Don's values were so different from those of most people that his words also could have a different meaning...Finally Hagen translated the question properly in his mind. Did Jack Woltz have the balls to risk everything, to run the chance of losing all on a matter of principle, on a matter of honor; for revenge?*

—*The Godfather*

There is one true hero in *The Godfather*: Enzo the baker, the stylized figure on the cover to whom this book is dedicated. At the hospital, Michael tells Enzo that he should leave, that there is going to be trouble. When the son of New York's most feared don says there's going be trouble, it means violence and possibly death. Out of gratitude and loyalty to the Godfather, with nothing to gain and everything to lose, Enzo stays. Plenty scared, he risks his life standing with Michael outside the hospital, two pretend sentries with pretend guns. They scare off Sollozzo's hitmen sent to murder the Don. Enzo has real balls.

When confronted with fight or fold on a matter of principle, most people fold. The percentage who will risk anything, much less everything, is tiny. The percentage of the time when such an effort results in anything but pain is even tinier.

They call the ability to divine what you can change and what you can't wisdom. The tough part about wisdom is that it's acquired through experience, much of which is mistakes and failures. There seems to be no substitute for trial and error—you don't progress unless you fail on occasion. Show me someone who's never failed and I'll show you someone's who's never going to succeed.

Wisdom comes to those who seek it. Leave yourself open to the new and novel, ask questions, listen more than you speak, seek the truth, don't worry about the impression you're making, don't fear failure, strive for integrity, and learn from your inevitable mistakes and your store of wisdom will know increase and plenty.

You'll need it. My gut instincts and firmly held belief in the law of consequences say that we're heading towards epic hard times the likes of which few of us have ever experienced. They'll require every ounce of courage, resourcefulness, integrity and wisdom we have.

Chapter 12

The Soul of Michael Corleone

Michael stands at a window looking out on Lake Tahoe and hears the shot that kills his brother. Fredo had been fishing with Al Neri, his murderer. For luck he recited the *Hail Mary*, a self-administered last rite. Every known enemy of Michael and the Corleone family is now dead. The last three to die—Hyman Roth, Frank Pentangeli, and Fredo—were more irritants than threats. Roth and Pentangeli would have died in prison. Fredo was a prisoner on Michael's estate. Michael bows his head.

Part Two ends with a close-up of him seated outside amidst the pines. He holds his half-clenched hand to his mouth in a contemplative pose.

He is a man with everything. Having outsmarted a congressional committee and embarrassed its members, no politician or other official will challenge him, cementing his position as the most powerful Mafia figure in the country. His wealth and business interests, both legitimate and illegitimate, are vast. He resides in his magnificent Lake Tahoe compound and perhaps equally plush residences elsewhere. Senator Patrick Geary and Connie Corleone, who both incurred Michael's displeasure in the movie's opening scenes, are now faithful lap dogs.

He is a man with nothing. All he can expect from other people is deference born of fear. Who will challenge a man who killed his brother and brother-in-law, and drained the vitality and life from his sister? His orders will be obeyed, the flattery will be endless, and he will dominate every relationship. Kay saw it first but other women, the kind of intelligent and independent women he once found desirable, will see it too: there's nothing left in Michael to love. Any relationships in the future will be with women who are drawn to money and power. Having struck the Faustian bargain in his father's hospital room, he's now hostage to that money and power, and to the criminality and violence that produced it. He's also hostage to the never-ending fear that plagues those with money and power: that he could somehow lose it all.

Michael has lost his soul. At the end of *Part Two*, he is bereft of that which makes humans human. You can see it in those cold, dark, impassive eyes. Whether he can ever regain his soul—his professed Christian doctrine holds out the hope that he can—is between him and his God.

After I parted company with the private partnership in Los Angeles, I was confronted with a profound issue. I could have looked for another job as a bond trader. However, I had come to question the value of my profession.

Don Corleone finally spoke to answer. "My friends,"
he said, "I didn't refuse out of spite. You all know me.
When have I ever refused an accommodation? That's
simply not in my nature. But I had to refuse this time.
Why? Because I think this drug business will destroy us
in the years to come...."

—The Godfather

As the Godfather believed drugs would destroy the Mafia, I believe debt will destroy the United States. Governments and their central banks have the power to conjure up debt at will. They can print currencies or make an entry on a computer screen and buy goods and services with the newly created paper or entry. It's the ultimate something-for-nothing racket. Government and central bank debt has become the foundation of the US and global economy.

Debt has the same addictive power as drugs. Increasing fixes of debt—borrowing from the future— are needed to maintain the same economic high. Government and central bank creation of debt and suppression of interest rates encourages individuals, companies, and state and municipal governments to borrow.

There is no way this ends well. Having borrowed so much from the future, the future cannot be anything but bleak. Sooner or later those who are obligated to repay the debt collapse under its weight, taking their creditors with them. Every perpetual-motion debt bubble eventually pops, leading to default, deflation, and depression, the size of which is directly related to the size of the bubble. We're in the biggest debt bubble in history. The coming depression will be one for the record books.

As a municipal bond trader, I made markets in municipal debt. In other words, I greased the skids for politicians and their constituents who were getting the benefits from that debt but obligating taxpayers, their children, grandchildren, and so on to repay it. Did I really want my tombstone to read: *Here lies Robert Gore, he helped governments go deeper into debt and turned future generations into debt slaves*?

No, I decided, I did not. You can't erase the past but you can try to atone for it. I had made a number of big trades in my career. Now I undertook an anti-big trade, one driven by conscience that entailed outsize risks with little probable gain or actual loss: I decided to write full-time.

I have always loved to write and self-published one book, *The Gordian Knot,* while I was still trading bonds. It was a good but not great book that had taught me a lot about writing a novel. I had completed the draft for my second novel, *The Golden Pinnacle*, when I left the bond business.

If everyone could experience the overwhelming emotional uplift I felt when I finished that draft the world would be a much better place. I had written it to my own standards and I knew that I had something that was good, very good. I didn't need or care about anyone else's evaluation of the book. I had accomplished what I had set out to accomplish as a writer: the purest, highest, and rarest joy, the joy of creating something its creator regards as great.

I went with my sister, who's a doctor and a good writer, to a writers' conference in Chicago. My sister has a neurotic obsession with the Cubs—I think all Cubs fans do—and I took her to a game (they lost). The conference attendees got to meet with prominent literary agents. I told the agent I met with about my book: the rags-to-riches story of a financial entrepreneur and his family during the Industrial Revolution. It depicts that time as an American golden age and champions freedom, capitalism, individualism, and honest money. After I finished editing and condensing the book I estimated it would be around 800 pages.

I give the agent credit, she knew her business and she was honest. She said it sounded like an interesting book, but her chances of selling it to the publishers she dealt with were zero. Unknown authors don't sell 800-page books and even well-known ones have trouble. The Industrial Revolution isn't exactly a hot period in the historical fiction market, there are almost no books set during that time. My themes and viewpoint wouldn't get much of a welcome in an industry dominated by political liberals. She asked if I had considered self-publishing.

I had. Nothing she said surprised me, only that she was so forthright about it. She was my last real contact with the legacy publishing industry. After two years of editing and condensing and my exit from the bond business, I self-published *The Golden Pinnacle* in 2013. I've sold a fair number of paperback and Kindle editions, the reader reviews have been superlative, and my opinion of the book hasn't changed one bit. I self-published my next book, *Prime Deceit,* a political satire and also a very good book, and I'm self-publishing this one.

Writing has been the quintessential anti-big trade with the expected minimal monetary payoff, but a huge spiritual one. I've written what I wanted to write and I haven't sold my soul to the publishing industry. I don't confine my books to its genre straightjackets. My next book is never going to be just like my last book, only a little different. I haven't hedged my political viewpoints at all. I don't have a social media platform. I don't do book signings or attend trade shows. If all this means that I'm writing for "The Remnant," the classic term from Albert Jay Nock's essay *Isaiah's Job,* then so be it.

Writing my books and my website, straightlinelogic.com, has been the most intrinsically satisfying thing I've ever done—it's never seemed like work—and it's had marvelous fringe benefits. I've met some great people through my writing. I've given speeches in various venues to interesting groups. I'm not going to change the world, but I think I've moved the needle in some small way. Call it partial atonement for my career as a merchant of debt.

Further atonement may be in the offing through the startup. Our technologies can cut the materials and energy used in a variety of applications while reducing environmental harms and safety and health risks. In addition to being green that way, they're going to be green as in profits, perhaps substantially so. There's nothing wrong and much that is right about that. Run, don't walk, from those who disparage honest profits; they're up to no good.

The *Capo dei Capi* and the *pezzonovantis* have brought about the terrible evil that engulfs the world. Soulless, they watch us through cold, dark, impassive eyes. They have it all and they have nothing. Present political arrangements—the governments and string-pullers who have enslaved us—aren't worth lifting a finger to save. They in fact must be resisted and fought at every turn, their downfall hastened in every way possible. A silver lining in the coming depression is that it will take down governments and obliterate current political boundaries.

There are principles worth fighting and dying for: freedom, individual rights—including the right to peacefully and honestly live one's life as one sees fit—protecting those rights for all, and voluntary and peaceful interaction among people. Whatever the flaws of the American founders and the system they set up, they had balls. They pledged their lives, their fortunes, and their sacred honor to their cause. In many cases they lost one or both of the first two, which burnished the last one.

You can stand for what you believe in and fight for it or you can take the path of no resistance and fold, but you cannot avoid the choice.

It's your choice. It's your life. It's your soul.

About the Author

Robert Gore grew up in Los Alamos, New Mexico. He graduated from UCLA with degrees in political science and economics, *Summa Cum Laude* and *Phi Beta Kappa*. He graduated from UC Berkeley with Master of Business Administration and *Juris Doctor* degrees, passed the California bar exam, and is an inactive member of the California Bar.

Mr. Gore traded primarily municipal bonds for three different firms for twenty-eight years. He was a partner at Crowell, Weedon & Co., where he worked for twenty-two years until 2012, and was director of the fixed income department and member of the executive committee. Since 2012 he has devoted his time to writing. Since 2016 he has also been involved as an investor and executive for 4Ry Inc., a technology startup (4rysprays.com).

The Gordian Knot, a legal thriller and Mr. Gore's first novel, was published in 2000. *The Golden Pinnacle*, a work of historical fiction, was published in 2013, and *Prime Deceit*, a political satire, in 2016. All three novels are available on Amazon. Mr. Gore's website is straightlinelogic.com, where he posts his own and other writers' articles about current events, literature and history. His articles have been reposted on Zero Hedge, David Stockman's Contra Corner, Lew Rockwell, The Burning Platform, Western Rifle Shooter's Association, and numerous other websites. He has done a variety of speaking engagements and media appearances.

Mr. Gore plays golf, skis, swims, and cycles. Although he writes political commentary, he enthusiastically shuns politics.

Made in the USA
Coppell, TX
23 December 2022

90629167R00095